For Diana

Contents

We talked far into the night, as friends do when they meet again, amid the homely village smells.

'How long have you been hearing confessions?'

'About fifteen years. . . .'

'What has confession taught you about men?'

'Oh, confession teaches nothing, you know, because when a priest goes into the confessional he becomes another person — grace and all that. And yet. . . . First of all, people are much more unhappy than one thinks . . . and then. . . .'

He raised his brawny countryman's arms in the starlit night:

'And then, the fundamental fact is that there is no such thing as a grown-up person. . . .'

ANDRÉ MALRAUX — *Antimemoirs*

Acknowledgements

I want to thank Eric Rayner, Naomi Stadlen and Catherine Storr for their helpful comments on an early draft, and Ben Churchill, with whom I have discussed the main theme of the book at length and whose ideas have made a significant contribution to what I have written.

For permission to use copyright material acknowledgement is made to the following:

Anne Allen and *Books for Your Children* for the untitled poem by a child.

Jonathan Cape and Princeton University Press for a quotation from the poem 'Mr Stratis Thalassinos Describes a Man' by George Seferis, translated by Edmund Keeley and Philip Sherrard in *Collected Poems 1924–55*.

Faber & Faber Ltd and Oxford University Press Inc. (New York) for the poem 'The Child Dying' by Edwin Muir in *Collected Poems*.

The Hogarth Press and Harcourt Brace Jovanovich Inc., for the poem 'Walls' by C. P. Cavafy, translated by Rae Dalven in *The Complete Poems of Cavafy* (copyright 1949 by Rae Dalven).

Houghton Mifflin Company (Boston) for quotations from *Client-Centered Therapy* by Carl R. Rogers.

Routledge & Kegan Paul for a passage from *Phenomenology of Perception* by M. Merleau-Ponty.

I wish to make acknowledgement to the editor of *New Society* for an extract from my article 'In Defence of Psychotherapy', to the editor of the *New Statesman* for modified extracts from my

A*

book reviews of *Attachment and Loss* by John Bowlby and *Motherhood and Personality* by L. Chertok, and to the editor of the *New York Times* for a modified extract from my book review of *Erik H. Erikson* by Robert Coles.

Introduction

The mind has a thousand eyes,
And the heart but one;
Yet the light of a whole life dies
When love is done.
F. W. BOURDILLON

This book is about psychotherapy, although I shall not restrict myself to the encounters that take place within the walls of a consulting-room.

During the course of writing the book I have become increasingly less inclined to view the psychotherapeutic process as a medical or scientific endeavour. It is, I believe, less a matter of applying a technique than forming a relationship, less an attempt to treat a sick person than to find one's way through the false ways in which a person may live, and help him to experience his life more truly. This is not to imply that the psychotherapist should preoccupy himself primarily with people who are clearly seeking for the true meaning of life and ignore the vast majority of the mentally ill, but it encompasses the view that the therapist and his patient are obliged to undertake this kind of search, in greater or lesser degree, if a fruitful outcome is to be expected.

These two facts about the nature of psychotherapy complement each other. If its aim is to reveal the patient's capacity to experience life in a real way, then one can only expect this to happen if the therapist himself acts in the encounter as a real person : true experience has little chance of emerging in a false setting.

Yet I believe the traditional psychiatric – and even psycho-analytical – approach to disturbed people contains elements which severely limit and often completely prevent the tender growth of a true experience which has already received dis-appointments and reversals before professional help is sought out.

Before discussing this matter any further I would like to report two extracts from psychotherapeutic sessions. They are taken from the first two of my sessions with patients today and therefore, not being carefully selected, are likely to be reason-ably typical.

The first was with a middle-aged woman who had three children. She reported an event that had occurred over the weekend. A friend had invited her to her home for the day but had included only one of the children in the invitation. 'Does she think children are just like numbers?' she said angrily. 'Children are individuals.'

I made the comment that she herself had, in childhood, felt she was not treated as an individual whose wishes and interests counted, and went on to note that she consistently anticipated that I would treat her in a similarly mechanical way, not seeing her as a unique person but as merely one patient among others.

She agreed that she did expect this of me; then she returned to the subject of her childhood, remembering how her parents had reacted to her games and productions with a well thought-out response, given in their own good time. It was unlike the present situation with her own children, in which there was an immediate and spontaneous interchange of comment and feeling.

The second patient was a man in his twenties who, as was characteristic of him, lay on the couch motionless and talked in a withdrawn and rather hopeless way about his loneliness. At one point in the session I said : 'Don't you think that I, too, might be lonely? Here I am sitting with you in this room and you are withdrawn from me. Don't you recognize that I don't want this, that I want to get to know you better?'

Patient: 'No, how could you? I can't believe it. You are self-sufficient. You don't want *me*.'

Me: 'What makes you think I'm self-sufficient? Why should I be different from you? I need people like you do. And I need you to stop keeping away from me.'

Patient: 'What could *I* give you? I can't imagine it. It's ridiculous. I feel so much a nothing. I never do anything in my life.'

Me: 'But in any case one doesn't like people just because of their achievements, but because of what they are. Don't you?'

Patient: 'Yes. That's true for me.'

Me: 'So why don't you believe that other people might like *you* for what you are?' . . .

At the end of the session he smiled in a warmer way than usual. 'It's a hard world,' he said.

The following observations occur to me about these extracts.

They are concerned with love. One could think of the phenomena in theoretical terms of various kinds (a Freudian psychoanalyst might, for instance, consider the patient's urges to derive from an instinctual desire for physical gratification) to explain love, but such deductions, even if correct, would be irrelevant. I could deduce the existence of a wish to seduce me in some way or to rival my other patients, and so on, but to do so would introduce factors of secondary importance. What these patients were speaking of was – irreducibly – love.

It was made explicit by the first patient that worthwhile love was spontaneous and saw the other in his uniqueness.

It was believed – by the second patient – that the only kind of love available to him was a conditional one; that he had to earn it by achievement, that he would not be loved for himself alone. Both patients, it seemed to me, felt sad, or cynical, about the fact that, in their experience, love was conditional: that it was given only if one behaved well or only in stereotyped, formal ways.

The patients are bringing to me, of their own volition, basic problems of living; first and foremost, of love; and I am trying to understand and help them. In doing so I bring to bear (implicitly or explicitly) my own philosophy of living. For instance, I assume that it is better to be in communication with people than withdrawn from them.

I do not speak, or think, in terms of an illness which has to be cured. I am not attempting to classify, make a prognosis or form a plan of treatment. What I am doing has little in common with traditional medical treatment.

I am – as far as I consciously know – truthful in these situations: that is to say, I don't lie, humour, or attempt to confuse.

In neither example do I reveal special skill, knowledge, or insight. Yet I am not ashamed of my responses. They seem to me to show a certain amount of understanding of human nature and to be reasonably appropriate.

If I made a mistake it was, I think, more likely to be due to a human error than a failure of something that could be called a technique. For instance, on reflection, it seems to me that in the first case laziness or conservatism may have led me into the easy path of uninvolved interpretation whereas in the second case my impatience might have forced the patient into a conformist response which did not come from the heart.

My own responses in the two examples are, in one respect, rather different. In the first, I reveal my feelings only implicitly, if at all, whereas in the second I declare them much more openly. (I refer here to the words spoken, which are the only data I am giving. My non-verbal behaviour – my tone of voice, etc. – would be difficult to convey accurately in print. It was, so far as I can tell, much as one might expect from the verbal report: that is to say, for instance, my voice showed more feeling and urgency in the second interchange.)

I feel less easy at reporting the latter example. Whereas in the former I could, if I chose, think of myself as a professional person, standing back in a detached and objective manner that would remain true to my training as a scientist, a doctor, a Freudian psychoanalyst (and, behind that, probably, a male who grew up in England as a member of the lower middle class), in the latter I am no longer an observer. I make an appeal – an appeal to the patient to change and an appeal that he consider me as a person. I reveal something of my nature and I show emotion.

My behaviour is perhaps best described as an ordinary human response to a person in trouble. This is not a response, however, that the two patients expect. They assume that I am a professional person whose feelings are not aroused by them, who is – at least in this context, but not only in this context – above the kind of feelings through which they are so tormented. I am, in their eyes, different from them; there is a gulf between us: the therapist and his patient, the well and the sick, the serene and the disturbed, the helper and the helped, the loved and the unloved. In the second case I am impelled to challenge this preconception. The patient's response, at the end of the session – 'It's a hard world' – suggests to me that my challenge had made some impression on his previous assumption. He did not say it in a tone which meant 'It's a hard world for poor, unhappy me', but 'It's a hard world, isn't it, for me and you and others who live in it?' It was a recognition of our mutual frailty and ordinariness. This, to my mind, is the crux of the matter. Unless there is an acceptance by the therapist of equality with his patient, the undertaking is jeopardized from the start. Nothing is easier than to say that one treats other people whose status is in some way inferior to one's own (as, for instance, Pupil/Teacher or Boss/Worker) as an equal, and nothing is easier than to write a book saying that one treats one's patients as equals. But the ways in which one person confers inferiority on another are legion and infinitely subtle and are not incompatible with what is usually called a 'kind' or 'humane' approach to the other person. My primary aim in this book is to explore and discuss some of the ways in which a harmful inequality between parent and child leads to false ways of experiencing life which later may be adjusted in a psychotherapeutic setting. This will involve, at times, explorations into the theoretical frameworks upon which psychiatry and psychoanalysis have been built. A further point. If what I am doing is *ordinary*, is it of use, and if it is, then how? Why report it? Who wants to know about ordinary behaviour? Were it not for the fact that I am a professional – an expert or specialist who is supposed to be qualified in some way to cure people – I would not have been invited to write this book. (I would not feel justified, for instance, in giving an account of how I bring up my children or make love to my wife – unless I had literary powers and were to disguise it all in a novel – as though I was specially clever in these matters, an example of excellence to put before others less clever and good.) It is necessary here to attempt to clarify what I mean by ordinary.

Each person develops special interests and skills and may take up a special type of work. In health, however, his sense of identity and perceptual stance remains primarily based on the fact that he is an ordinary human being, made of the same stuff as his fellow men, capable of understanding and being understood. If – perhaps as a form of defence against accepting what he is – he comes to identify himself primarily with a certain characteristic or function (as, for instance, an official may equate his rank with his worth) he has, to that extent, become alienated from his ordinary self.

Those who seek out help from a psychotherapist have, in some way and in some degree, lost their capacity for ordinary living. They have come to regard themselves as special, an experience that is painful either because they feel too odd or wicked or stupid to be understood by an ordinary person, or because they feel that those around them are quite unable to appreciate their real nature: they are in a special position in that they cannot share their experience in the way that seems possible for most people. (In both cases a compensation may set in, resulting in the idealization of this specialness, as in the fantasy of being God, Christ, or Napoleon.) The help that is needed is the restoration of the patient's sense of being an ordinary person, potentially acceptable and understandable.

It would seem reasonable to suppose that this restoration would most readily take place in an atmosphere of ordinariness; in a relationship in which the patient feels valued for his ordinary human qualities, those which he shares with the rest of mankind : fundamentally, his capacity to experience. And in order to value him for these qualities the other person must have them and show that he has them : he must be an ordinary human being; he must not conceal his frailty.

In so far as the psychotherapist sets himself apart from his patient, giving the impression – even if only implicitly, by reticence – that he is a different order of being, his capacity to heal is reduced. Several arguments can be put against this.

Firstly, the therapist needs to remain detached in order to protect himself and his patient from too disturbing an emotional involvement.

Secondly, the therapist needs to remain detached in order to perceive the patient more clearly (more scientifically).

Thirdly, the therapist needs to remain detached in order to be a blank screen on which the patient can project his fantasies.

Fourthly, the therapist acts, in the psychotherapeutic setting, as a specialist. This does not imply that he is not also an ordinary human being nor that his attitude to the patient lacks humanness.

None of these objections are, to my mind, valid. The first three I shall discuss in Chapters 5 and 8; the last I shall concern myself with now.

The therapist does, indeed, have special experience. He is accustomed – unless an absolute beginner – to being in the presence of troubled people and trying to help them. One would expect him to have learned something from this and therefore to be able to give more help than the average man-in-the-street. However, although this is true – and is, indeed, the chief justification for anyone's calling himself a psychotherapist – it is a less telling point than appears at first sight. Helping troubled people is not so specialized an occupation as many others (such as surgery). It is the main burden of the work of many people – such as mothers, social workers, clergymen – who do not regard themselves as psychotherapists, and it forms an important part of ordinary living: from infancy onward people are troubled and those around them learn ways of helping. The skill required to help a troubled person is one that is primarily learned in the school of ordinary living. The most a psychotherapeutic training centre can hope to achieve is to attract those suited to the work and increase their capacity to do it. It can do this by making the trainee aware of the false ways in which he characteristically behaves towards people. It can help him avoid taking up the false roles, including that of a specialist, into which he might be attracted or seduced. It can, in other words, help him to be ordinary and to remain so in difficult circumstances. In doing this it would forewarn him that the therapeutic endeavour cannot be expected to be less difficult and demanding than are all other intimate relationships that occur in one's life. By far the most important element in such a training is to give the pupil an opportunity to experience for himself the help that is possible in a psychotherapeutic encounter – a fact which has been recognized by most training centres since the work of Freud. The two most serious hazards of this procedure are, firstly, that the pupil may be unable to reveal himself openly to the training therapist for fear of being considered unworthy to qualify, and secondly, that he may emerge as a graduate from the institute with the belief that the prime purpose of his experience has been the acquisition of a special technique.

The burden of what I am saying is this – once the psychotherapeutic situation is conceived in more differentiated and formal terms than 'Here is A trying to help B', there is a danger of a gulf developing between the two people which all the training and technique in the world will not bridge. The significant characteristic of the psychotherapeutic situation is that it is, or should be, a place where it is possible to be ordinary in a society that for the most part requires people to relate to each other by means of special roles, as for instance – doctor and patient, social worker and client. To put it another way, all situations, at least all that I can think of, involve some specialization of function. This diminishes experience only if undertaken defensively (as a flight from the ordinary) or if it involves such preoccupation that a truly balanced vision of life becomes impossible. The forces that have moulded contemporary psychiatry and psychotherapy have, I believe, made it very difficult for two people to meet each other to discuss, in a natural and ordinary way, the problems of one of them.

If the main argument of this book appears rather obvious to some readers, I would ask them to look at it as a record of my attempt to escape from the obscurities of a speciality into the common light of day. And if the language that I use is simple, this is not out of a desire to avoid complexity, but because I believe that ordinary language is the most adequate means available to convey the facts of human experience. I would, for the most part, use the same language if I were writing a paper for a professional journal.

Although the traditional approach to mental disturbance is still dominant in our society, it has met with severe criticism in recent years. The most forceful and cogent of this criticism takes a form, in Britain at least, which is characteristic of that radical opposition to established values known as the 'counter-culture' or 'alternative society', and constitutes not only a critique of the impersonality of contemporary psychiatry but a rejection of the concept of mental illness and the assertion of a theory of the origin of so-called mental illness which involves an indictment of the family as we know it. Despite a large measure of sympathy towards this movement, I believe it to constitute an ideology which is at variance with the psycho-therapeutic aims described above: in particular, that it does not come to terms with the acceptance of ordinariness, with the natural need for dependence, and with the capacity for love which exists in families as we know them. During the course of this book I have tried to find my way into a critique of impersonal approaches to mental pain which does not involve me in a cynical and unrealistic view of traditional morality and contemporary family life. In what follows I shall contrast the established and the *avant-garde* (or, what may be called the scientific–rationalist and existential–pheno-menological) viewpoints from various angles, attempting to assess the ways in which each has a partial hold on the truth. In the latter part of the book I shall discuss some aspects of the origin and nature of psychological disturbance, and finally return to my point of departure: the practice of psychotherapy.

One should perhaps not try too hard to forestall adverse comment but I would like at this point to confront one criticism to which my view of psychotherapy is open.

In maintaining that psychotherapy is an experience which has more in common with the ordinary intimate relationships of life than with the special techniques of science, I do not discount the knowledge of life obtained by or through techni-cal procedures. This knowledge is of two kinds. In the first case it consists of those methods of investigation and treatment of human suffering – such as 'organic psychiatry' – which are quite distinct from the therapeutic encounter. In this book I am only concerned with these methods in so far as they have been allowed to impinge improperly on the practice of psycho-therapy. In the second case this knowledge comes from the techniques employed by psychotherapists themselves and com-monly considered by them to constitute the essence of their endeavours. These techniques are valid methods of exploration provided they are seen as aids to communication between therapist and patient and not regarded as the *sine qua non* of the relationship. Furthermore I recognize – indeed, it is obvious – that however limiting is the technical procedure of psychotherapy, it has in this century been the means by which a large number of people have been rescued from the tyranny of their neuroses and have truly found themselves. But this fact does not entirely vindicate the procedure; the achievement may in large part be due to the fact that the humanness of both therapist and patient has transcended the limitation of the method. True being is not easily extinguished; a little increase in life-space – even in flawed conditions – can be enough for growth to start again.

2
The Nature of Illness

Nasrudin was sedately riding his donkey along the road when it suddenly reared and he fell off. A group of small boys playing surrounded him and almost split their sides with laughter.

When they had wiped the tears from their eyes Nasrudin sat up, and adjusted his turban with unruffled dignity.

'And what do you think you are laughing at?'

'Mulla,' they said, chortling at the memory, 'it was a wonderful sight! We were laughing at you falling off your donkey.'

'You have not taken into consideration,' said Nasrudin, 'the possibility that I might have had a reason for falling!'

IDRIES SHAH,
The Pleasantries of the Incredible Mulla Nasrudin

A person who seeks the help of a psychotherapist may or may not consider himself ill. Whether he does so or not is irrelevant to the issue and would never need to be discussed were it not that the concept of illness is the subject of so much confusion and corruption that it often forces itself into the thoughts of those who need help. Let me give two examples.

A patient was talking about his 'depression'. After a while I said 'You feel despair, don't you?'

'That's it,' he replied gratefully. 'It's despair. That *means* something to me.'

Whereas 'depression' was a meaningless illness, despair was the natural response to an accumulation of the failure, guilt and confusion of a human being.

After I had been seeing a woman patient for some time she mentioned that the sexual relationship with her husband was virtually non-existent. I expressed surprise she had not mentioned this fact before. 'But I put it down to the illness,' she said, 'no one who feels as ill as I do would want sex.' There is a sense in which this is true, but in thinking of the illness as an entity in itself she has failed to recognize the contribution which her sexual problems made towards the feeling of illness.

These two examples reveal ways in which the concept of illness led the 'sick' person to think of himself in a rigid and unimaginative manner and interfered with his capacity to understand his disability. It is, however, the tendency to place himself and be placed in a category of persons which distinguishes and alienates him from the (supposedly healthy) psychiatrist which is probably the most dangerous consequence of using the term. This alienation, which can so easily involve complacency on the part of the therapist and envy on the part of the patient, seriously limits the amount of healing that can take place. But first : what is illness?

In health a person lives freely and is able to accomplish all those aims which lie within the boundaries of his (intrinsic) capacity and the limitations put upon him by his environmental circumstances. Illness is the term which has come to be used to describe the state of a person whose capacity to function is in some way lessened, who cannot confront the challenges around him as adequately as before. Something has got the better of him. It may be a destructive invasion from outside, as when he takes in a toxic quantity of typhoid bacteria, or it could be a breakdown of his normal functioning due to wear and tear, as, for instance, the rupture of an intracranial artery whose lining was unduly weak at a certain point. We base our conclusion that a person is ill on the fact that he is not merely a victim of an adverse situation which has interfered with his capacity to act, but that a change has taken place in him which prevents his action even if environmental conditions are favourable. A man pinned to the ground by a fierce Alsatian dog is incapacitated but not ill. If the dog is then removed by its owner the man will be regarded as ill only if he is unable to respond to the now favourable conditions either because he is too shocked or because the dog has bitten him. Like most distinctions this one is not always easy to maintain, but it is a commonly accepted usage, which I shall adhere to in this chapter.

As I have defined it – and in the ordinary and dictionary usage of the term – the state of illness does not necessarily involve a comparison with other people. A sick man is 'not himself': the measure of his failure is his own usual healthy state. This is true even with those signs of illness for which medicine has established a recognized and quantifiable norm for the healthy average population. If a person is found to have a resting pulse-rate of 85 the precise significance of this finding is dependent on a knowledge of his pulse-rate when healthy. Because his doctor does not usually have this information he uses as his criterion the figure believed to be average for the population and accepted as healthy by the medical profession, hoping that in this particular case it will be near enough an approximation to the truth to make a correct diagnosis. Fortunately, it usually is. And with the proliferation of complicated laboratory investigations the justification for relying on a standard norm for comparison has become even greater. But this practice has, I think, had the effect of subtly altering our concept of health, the customary criterion now being : do we measure up to the rest of the population, i.e. the ideally healthy person in the doctor's mind?

A further reason for what might be called the objectivication of the concept of illness is the increasing reliance on diagnostic categories of illness – on the refinement of the doctor's ability to identify an actual affliction in terms of a distinct clinical entity. No medical student nowadays would dare suggest to his professor that a certain patient was merely 'run down' or suffering from 'indigestion'; the condition would have to be fitted into a recognized category of disease as specified in the textbooks. Although it is undoubtedly helpful to know that a disease called measles exists and has certain signs, symptoms and causes, this technical knowledge draws attention away from the person himself and the characteristics and vicissitudes of his own peculiar states of health and sickness. It has seduced the medical profession into believing that the classifications useful for diagnosis necessarily correspond to distinctions in the natural world. The degree to which our conceptions truly represent the actual things they are supposed to is, of course, open to debate. It would, however, seem useful to make a distinction here between those diagnostic categories which force themselves upon us (as, for instance, measles) and those which arise from our own need to classify. Whereas the former are pragmatically true and give rise to little confusion, the latter are, at best, convenient terms for specialists exploring the nature of certain disabilities, and at worst, artificial and misleading – products of a rigid need to control reality by compartmentalization.

The objectivication of illness, involving an excessive reliance on classification and standardized data, has led to mistakes in the field of physical medicine, as for instance the former tendency to diagnose organic heart disease in patients who would now be regarded as suffering from physiological malfunctioning of the (organically healthy) heart because of psychological stress. It is, however, in the field of mental health that this tendency has had the most serious consequences, one of which is the current confusion about the nature, or even the existence, of 'mental illness'.

Traditional medicine restricts the concept of illness to those forms of it which seize upon the person and impose their own pattern upon his life (I shall term these 'mechanical' as opposed to 'meaningful' illnesses); and, when studying disability, focuses on the aspects which best fit this kind of approach. Thus the doctor is not interested in the pattern which the patient himself may impose upon the illness. When I get measles I may take it like a man or I may whine and moan about my condition; I may, in convalescence, read *Tiger Tim's Annual* or *Finnegans Wake*, but the doctor is unlikely to record this in his notes or put it into his textbooks; rather he will note the distribution of my spots, over which, so far as I know, I have no control.

In focusing attention on these aspects of illness, medicine is working on the implicit assumption that it is an unfortunate and meaningless interruption of the normal state of health, an event not only unrelated, for the most part, to the person's total existence, and unpatterned by his personality, but an unmitigated failure of adaptation from which no benefit can be expected. But is this assumption an appropriate one?

If we approach the question of illness as though it were an emanation of the patient's being, an expression of his aims and a meaningful aspect of his total life situation, certain different ways of understanding this illness are open to us.

Firstly, the illness may be a consequence of over-exertion of some kind. A person may, for some reason (which itself might be a manifestation of illness), try to do things which are so beyond his capacity that he breaks down under the strain : he may undergo a general collapse, or an organ of his body which has perhaps been subject to particular strain may cease to function adequately. In this event the pattern of the illness bears no intrinsic relation to his general aims in life and does not *directly* express a particular conflict that he has been experiencing; it is not wanted and has come upon him like an act of God. His only contribution has been, knowingly or unknowingly, to put himself at greater risk than the ordinary course of living should require.

Secondly, a person's aims may be so confused and unco-ordinated that this manifests itself openly in disability. Because of, say, an ambiguous attitude to authority, he may develop a stutter or a catatonic stupor or an irregularity of heart-beat in all situations in which a question of authority plays a part. This paralysis of action is not something that he intended, and can be regarded as accidental and secondary to the dilemma, but the dilemma itself and all its constituents are meaningful expressions of the person's life situation and the diseased organ itself may be selected because it has a direct or symbolic relation to this situation. As in the first category (above), the illness is not sought. Should the original confusion itself be considered an illness? This may be just a question of verbal usage, but in keeping with my earlier formulation (page 23) I would say that to be confused is part of life and occurs in health; it is only when the confusion persists even in favourable circumstances and becomes incapacitating that it merits the status of illness.

Thirdly, a person may take on a sick role purposely, using whatever methods are appropriate to achieve it consciously or unconsciously, for constructive or destructive ends. In this case the particular form of the illness is secondary to the fact of illness itself. The illness developed will be, ideally, the one most likely to gain acceptance as bona fide in the eyes of those around the patient, will depend on his knowledge and beliefs about various medical syndromes, and will be subject to the fashions of the day. If his aim is conscious he will be said to be a 'malingerer'; if not, a 'neurotic' or 'hysteric'.

A person who seeks illness in this way may do so for a variety of reasons : as a temporary or permanent escape from an intolerable situation; a shrinking back from active living; a method of indirect attack on others; a retreat from the ordinary pressures of life in order to achieve the only means of making a certain type of growth; or, more usually, a mixture of these and yet other motives. In so far as some of these motives are creative, or that illness, once established, may be used constructively (history and literature abound with striking examples – such as that of Ignatius Loyola or Ivan Ilych – of this phenomenon), illness is not necessarily – as in the traditional medical model – an unmitigated bad event.

Indeed, one might ask : is the person who purposely enters the sick role really sick? Once again we are involved in a question of semantics. But the answer seems to me to rest on the question of authenticity. One has to ask the kind of questions that one asks people in all spheres of life in order to establish whether the role they are adopting is genuine. Are they serious and committed or are they acting a part just for a bit of fun, as a form of distraction, or making a pretence which they hope will be exposed and for which the best response is 'Come off it'? Or have they decided that the only way out of a dilemma – the only hopeful path to take – is to temporarily enter a phase of illness?

Finally – and, for the most part, this concerns illnesses termed 'mental' – a person who is not ill in any of the above senses may mistakenly or intentionally be deemed ill by those around him and forced into a sick role. If a person's behaviour deviates sufficiently from that which society considers normal he may be placed into a subgroup to distinguish him from the majority, in order that he may be understood and related to more easily: he may be thought of as sick, mad, evil, blessed, possessed, criminal, and so on. Whereas most of the terms which society uses to categorize people – such as husband, wife, soldier, farmer – bear sufficient relationship to reality to be workable, those connoting and denoting deviance – mental case, criminal, et cetera – seem to run into trouble, to be vague, ambiguous and unduly subject to corruption and the changes of fashion. Consequently there is a danger that many people who are not sick may be thought to be. This group is likely to include those whose particular constellation of potentialities and limitations is merely unusual. They find it more difficult than most to adapt to the requirements of a society whose organization focuses on the average and which, for reasons of financial economy, cannot provide for the needs of those who are unusual. Such people are often more inclined than most to conflict and illness – for society accommodates more easily to the average – but are not inherently 'sick', and may, in some cases, be reasonably considered to be more vital and healthy than those of their fellows who find it easier to adapt to the crippling restrictions of a society which has lost touch with biological reality. For instance, in a study of mothering I came to the conclusion that in some cases a mother's ability to perceive the emotional needs of her baby – itself a strength – increased the risk of her succumbing to a post-natal breakdown.[1]

The wrongful attribution of illness to a healthy person may sometimes, however, be less a simple misperception than a calculated attempt to dominate or denigrate a person. To place someone in an inferior category is a widespread and effective method of ruling over him. It can be applied in general and particular ways. In the general form a whole class of persons – women, Negroes, Communists, Jews, etc. – are explicitly or implicitly proclaimed inferior by those in power, and thereafter regarded as being intrinsically unworthy and incapable of full citizenship. In the particular form a certain person may be placed in an inferior category to discredit him, as, for instance, when a public figure who justifiably opposes a move by the British or American governments is called a Communist, thereby identifying his judgement as that of an inferior and discredited group.

Both types of categorization can be, and are, applied to sickness. The sick, both mental and physical, as a class, tend to be considered inferior.[2] Patients are subject to the authority of a person (the doctor) of very high prestige, before whom they are obliged to humble themselves. This traditional differentiation of status – which varies directly in proportion to the degree of incapacity of the patient – is a powerful one, and it needs remarkable tenacity on the part of reformers aware of the psychological disadvantages to the patient to change it. The reason behind this attitude is primarily that the sick are in a weak position and, by their incapacity, present practical and moral problems to the strong, one solution of which fact is to deem them, as a class, inferior, from which it follows that their rights can be taken away and they can be segregated from the rest of society.

Once the category of sick persons exists as an inferior group then it can be utilized in the control of a particular person. Anyone – child or adult – who manifests behaviour which is an embarrassment or challenge to those around him may be labelled 'sick' (whether consciously or unconsciously) for the specific purpose of controlling, repressing and invalidating his ideas and actions. The most flagrant example of this at the present time is the incarceration in mental hospitals of some of the opponents of the Soviet régime. But there are examples nearer home. A child who refuses to go to school is nowadays said to be suffering from a neurosis called 'school-phobia'. By sending him to a Child Guidance Clinic the authorities do not need to confront the awkward question as to whether compulsory schooling is justified or try to improve school conditions.

In attempting to make a clear distinction between true illness and the wrongful attribution of illness, I have not yet commented on the relationship between these conditions. But, in practice, this may be close. A person who is wrongly considered ill is placed in a predicament which may well contribute to genuine illness. Not only are his social relations made (perhaps insuperably) difficult but his ability to perceive himself accurately comes under considerable strain. It is a situation in which vicious circles of various kinds can flourish. The situation is also complicated by the assumption that illness is a sign of inferiority, one result of which is that a genuinely sick person, who could overcome his illness in favourable circumstances, may be unable to withstand the designation of inferiority which his illness brings upon him.

In view of the enormous harm brought about by confusion between 'meaningful' and 'mechanical' illness, should the former continue to be termed 'illnesses'? Would it not be better to abandon the term and think up a new one?

For the kind of reasons I am stating here, terms such as 'mental illness', 'insanity', 'schizophrenia' have come under considerable criticism in recent years.[3,4] In calling attention to the confusion, these criticisms are necessary and important and help to restore the humanity of the patient – to bridge the crippling gulf between the 'sick' and the 'well'. But I do not think as yet a new formulation has appeared which does justice to the complexity of the problem. Such a formulation would, among other possible requirements, need to do the following:

Firstly, to describe the state of a person whose capacity for insight and potential for action is not necessarily less than those around him, yet, at the moment in question, needs looking after.

Secondly, it would need to avoid an overstatement of the case which results merely in a redistribution of the condition of 'illness' or 'inferiority'. This overstatement simply changes the sign, as it were : for instance, it is sometimes suggested that the patient is less sick than those around him (family, psychiatrists, society). Although there is a sense in which this may be true, for the patient is often trying to express a truth to which those around are blind, such a formulation does not convey that there is something wrong with the patient. Whatever the rights and wrongs of the situation and however sick those around him may be, he has reached such a state of pain, unhappiness, confusion and fatigue that he can no longer function in a healthy way.

Thirdly, it would have to recognize that, however different in origin and significance meaningful and mechanical illnesses are, they may take a similar form : they often feel the same, pass through similar stages, and require – in some ways – similar care. A person who has received a psychological shock may tremble, feel cold, take to his bed and need nursing in much the same way as someone who has succumbed to an infection.

Fourthly, it must include the fact that human anguish – the condition to which psychotherapists and allied workers apply themselves – does not necessarily present itself in a form to which the concept of illness can be usefully applied. There are people who can adapt to society and show no signs of illness, yet carry a deep hurt within themselves. Such people may – to the surprise of all who know them – commit suicide because their lives do not offer sufficient meaning.

But when all this is said, I believe the essential problem to lie within the area of comprehension at present designated 'moral'. As long as people continue to think of one another in terms of superiority and inferiority they will find categories to substantiate their belief, be it illness, I.Q., colour of skin or chromosome formation.

3
Perceptual Distortion in Contemporary Society and Psychiatry

The gentleman, after some silence, said to her: 'These heavy lorries they use here have too long a braking-distance.'

Somehow, the lady felt relieved at hearing this, and she thanked him with an attentive glance. Though she had doubtless heard the expression many times before, she did not know what a braking-distance was, nor had she any wish to know: it was sufficient for her that by this means the horrible happening could be fitted into some kind of pattern, so becoming a technical problem that no longer directly concerned her. And now the shrill whistle of an ambulance could be heard, and the promptness of its arrival was a source of satisfaction to the waiting crowd. How admirable these social institutions are!

ROBERT MUSIL, *The Man Without Qualities*

The dehumanizing factors in psychotherapeutic procedure, with which I am concerned in this book, are part of a view of man which dominates academic thinking.

In psychological literature the subjective, personal type of functioning has been regarded as less adequate, less true and less adult than the objective, impersonal. Even Piaget, who is a most sophisticated critic of the narrow conception of science embraced by most thinkers, writes in a way that suggests an overvaluation of objectivity :

Perception is essentially egocentric from every point of view : tied to the perceiver's position in relation to the object (centration) : it is strictly personal and incommunicable except through the mediation of language or of drawings, etc. This egocentricism is not only limiting but is also the source of systematic errors. . . . The essence of the operations of intelligence is, on the contrary, the achievement of knowledge, which is independent of the ego, independent of a particular individual's point of view (but not of human subjects in general, i.e. of activities common to a given level). Its essence is also the achievement of communicable or universal knowledge.[1]

Piaget follows the traditional approach in philosophy and psychology which places impersonal conceptual ways of patterning experience above personal ones. The impersonal approach ('intelligence') is, in his view, more correct, more mature than the personal; it is also more detached, being once removed from the original experience. This is an adult-centric view which idealizes a stereotype of mature functioning : calm, omniscient, unemotional detachment in contrast to the frantic and impulsive desires of the child; and the kind of adult it depicts has an obsessional character (albeit one that is acceptable as normal in our society) : he has sacrificed his passionate commitment to spontaneous living.

This conception of human nature is one aspect of the progressive dominance of the objective mode of functioning in Western society, a dominance which has been explored by several thinkers, notably Max Weber, who gave it the name of 'rationalization'. 'Rationalization' is

the product of the scientific specialisation and technical differentiation peculiar to Western culture. . . . It might be defined as the organisation of life through an exact study of men's relations with each other, with their tools and their environment for the purpose of achieving greater efficiency and productivity.[2]

Its aim, Weber believed, is perfectionist – the complete mastery of the external world – but, although it increases our capacity to handle many areas of living, our emotions remain irrational and not subject to its influence, and one of its disadvantages is that it diminishes the enchantment of the world. Weber was unable to account for the fact that rationalization is peculiar to Western civilization alone and even came up with the unlikely suggestion that it was a result of genetic endowment. But whatever the origin, the disease – social and philosophical obsessionality – is with us.

My own feeling is that it is, to some extent, the result of a vicious circle. Before man had developed efficient techniques to increase his safety and comfort, the attempt to control and plan his life was so likely to be in vain that it was hardly worth the effort. Once a certain threshold had been passed, the rewards of such effort became an ever-increasing inducement. The situation is rather like that of the person who does not think it worth trying to save money until his income is sufficiently secure to make a positive bank balance seem a real possibility. But such a person may eventually become a miser.

The industrial revolution not only accelerated the organization of society but precipitated socio-political philosophies which, from Bentham onwards, place value on a man for his capacity to organize himself to adapt to the system, rather than his simple capacity to *be*. Even the intellectual profundity of Marx, who sought to free man from the exploitation of his creative possibilities, failed to remedy the situation. It failed because, in laying such stress on work and organization in contemporary society, Marx fostered the development of a hierarchial system based on a person's ability to work with apparent potency. Marxism – whether we attribute it to defects in Marx's own thinking or a corruption of his thought – has not brought the promised equality. Thus, for example, Nadezhda Mandelstam writes, in her agonizing memoirs of life under Stalin :

I was sent back to the isolation hospital, where the use of germicides was unknown, except for patients belonging to the highest categories. Vishnevski happened to be in the hospital at the same time, and it was from him that I learned of the existence of new drugs which would have helped me recover much more quickly. But even the medicine you get depends on your status. I once complained about this in the presence of a Soviet official who had held high rank before his retirement. I said medicine was something everybody needed. 'What do you mean, everybody?' he asked. 'Do you expect me to get the same treatment as a cleaning woman?' He was a kind and perfectly decent person, but nobody was unaffected by the 'fight against egalitarianism'.[3]

It may be thought, cynically, that this kind of behaviour merely shows that man's innate greed will refute any ideology. But I believe this is not the whole truth, for a philosophy – such as contemporary Capitalism or Marxism – which over-values organization ability at the expense of creative freedom will inevitably foster competitive greed.

However, in order to gain a better understanding of the origin of excessive rationalization one has to consider the ways in which human beings distort reality. Within the limits of our innate mental equipment and our experience, we see the world more or less as it is. That is to say, our perception is sufficiently realistic to enable us to survive and enjoy living in an environment that is reasonably well attuned to our needs. But various things can happen to us during the course of our life which detract from this natural ability, so that our vision becomes, in some ways, distorted and our experience of life consequently falsified. Because life is not ideal this relative incapacity of vision is to some extent inevitable and not incompatible with what might be classed a normal state of health. But beyond a certain – albeit arbitrary – degree of falseness, we are sick : the meaning of life is diminished or even dies, however much this loss may be concealed beneath ingenious and often frantic attempts to persuade ourselves otherwise. Mental illness consists of the various modes of perceptual distortion undertaken by the human species and the equally varied techniques for concealing these distortions.

Perception has content and form, and either or both of these may be subject to distortion. For instance, content is distorted when a particular experience is denied. When a loved one dies the loss may be so intolerable to the survivor that he fails to perceive the occurrence and continues to believe, by means of a hallucination, that the loved one is still alive. If the need to distort is not so great, he may accept the physical occurrence, but deny its significance. Thus Tolstoy, on the death of his seven-year-old son, Vanishka, the gifted child on whom he had pinned great hopes, wrote in his diary : 'We have buried Vanishka. Terrible – no, not terrible; great spiritual event. I am grateful to you, Father, I am grateful to you.'

On the other hand the whole of the perceived world may be uniformly distorted so that although all objects are present they are seen in a peculiar light. In the rare condition known as micropsia, for instance, everything appears small. But perhaps the two most widespread forms of perceptual distortion are those of excessive objectivity (rationalization) considered above, and its counterpart, excessive subjectivity : these two forms roughly correspond to the mechanisms known to psychiatrists and psychoanalysts as 'obsessional' and 'hysterical'.

In subjective distortion things are perceived only in so far as they have a direct and immediate bearing on one's life; in objective distortion things are perceived only in terms of a general frame of reference. To give an example – on seeing a flower, the subjectifier will think 'This flower gives me (or does not give me) a good feeling', whereas the objectifier will think, 'This is a good (or bad) example of *sagittaria japonica*.' Neither of these two perceptions is false, but a person who habitually prefers to perceive within the context of one of these ways may, if he carries the business to excess, so miss out on the other aspect of experience that his overall picture of the world becomes falsified.

Subjective and objective perception are not equally relevant to all areas of experience; whereas the former is more appropriate when dealing with intimate relationships, the latter is of better use in bringing the inanimate and social world to order. As one might expect, therefore, women tend to be more fluent in the subjective realm, men in the objective.

The 'subjective' and 'objective' modes of perception are concepts which can be formulated in various ways (none of which are quite commensurate):

Subjective	Objective
Personal	Impersonal
Internal	External
Emotional	Intellectual
Fusing	Separating
Intuitive	Scientific
Limitless	Limited
Mystical	Materialistic
Romantic	Classical
Dionysian	Apollonian
Primary process	Secondary process*
Non-discursive	Discursive†
Syncretic	Analytic‡
Diverging	Converging§

How can the excessive objectivity (rationalization) which is the characteristic distortion of our time be cured? The greatest danger seems to me that the attempt at healing will result less in a return to true, undistorted vision than a substitution of another distortion. As every psychotherapist knows, one may cajole a patient to abandon one kind of defence against insight only to discover that he has produced an equally powerful (and usually complementary) one. Might this be

---

* Sigmund Freud, *Formulations on The Two Principles of Mental Functioning*, Standard Edition, vol 12, Hogarth Press (1958); and Charles Rycroft's elaboration of this theme, 'Beyond the Reality Principle' (*International Journal of Psychoanalysis*, 1962, 43, 388). Here Rycroft shows that these 'two principles' cannot be as sharply differentiated as Freud believed.

† Susanne Langer, *Philosophy in a New Key*, Harvard University Press, Cambridge, Massachusetts (1960).

‡ Anton Ehrenzweig, *The Hidden Order of Art*, Weidenfeld & Nicolson (1967).

§ J. W. Getzels and P. W. Jackson, *Creativity and Intelligence*, Wiley, New York (1962), elaborated by Liam Hudson in *Contrary Imaginations*, Penguin Books (1967).

happening to our society at present? The forces that oppose excessive objectivity are varied and relatively unorganized, but have recently been identified as the 'counter-culture'.[4] This movement is a revolt mainly by youth against the present power-structure of society; in particular it constitutes a determination to find a kind of experience other than that offered by the contemporary mode. For this reason it places itself in opposition to cognitive modes of expression, to science, material security and caution (such values are replaced by personal relationships and drugs which disable ordered thoughts), taking as its motto rather than rational moderation Blake's aphorism 'The road of excess leads to the palace of wisdom'; in so far as, rightly or wrongly, it equates the present concept of sanity with the narrow vision of rationality, it seeks 'madness'.

This protest is perhaps the healthiest and potentially most fruitful phenomenon of our time. It is the recognition that we are being spiritually strangled by obsessionality, in rather the same way that our environment is being destroyed by pollution, and that the problem is of comparable urgency: a recognition – rather similar to that made by Jesus Christ some time ago – that a return to a kind of simplicity is necessary for survival. But simplicity cannot easily be reached and many spokesmen of the movement go tumbling over in the direction of unlimited subjectivity. Here, for example, is Timothy Leary's celebration of the acid trip:

Ego cries, keep it on!
The glory of the psychedelic moment is the victory over life and death won by seeing the oscillating dance of energy and yielding to it.
The age-old appeal of the psychedelic experience is its solution to the problem of escape. The visionary revelation answers the escape question. There is no death. Ecstatic, mirthful relief. There is nothing to avoid, nothing to escape, nothing to fear. There is just off–on, in–out, start–stop, light–dark, flash–delay.
Death, void, oblivion, is the split second pause. I accept the on. I accept the off.[5]

In order to steel itself sufficiently for the task in hand, a movement of revolt must become preoccupied with the system it opposes, the better to understand it and define its opposition with the utmost vigour. But this preoccupation narrows its field of vision and makes creative perception difficult. The consequence is likely to be a continuous oscillation between extremes – in this case, between subjectivity and objectivity – rather than a new vision. However much one may regret the present domination of objectivity in contemporary society, the opposition brought to it must not itself be forced, by the heat of the struggle, into an alienated mode of perception.

Blake did not make this mistake himself, for he was aware of both possibility and limitation. Despite his exhortation to excess, he also wrote :

How do we distinguish the oak from the beech, the horse from the ox, but by the bounding outline? How do we distinguish one face or countenance from another, but by the bounding line and its infinite inflexions and movements? What is it that builds a house and plants a garden, but the definite and determinate? What is it that distinguishes honesty from knavery, but the hard and wiry line of rectitude and certainty in the actions and intentions? Leave out this line, and you leave out life itself; all is chaos again, and the line of the almighty must be drawn out upon it before man or beast can exist.

Quoted in Kathleen Raine, *William Blake*, Thames & Hudson (1970).

One of the temptations which lead us away from whole vision is the need to feel that we have it in our grasp. The true experience of life is infinitely varied and complex; one cannot stop life in midstream and formulate it in a phrase (even the phrase of a poet) or identify it in a feeling – to believe one can do so is the mistake of both the intellectual and the mystic. It is not, for instance, a calculated mean between the extremes I have discussed above. This is the misconception which lies at the heart of the Snow–Leavis controversy : one cannot make a man whole by teaching him a certain amount of science and a certain amount of art. The two extreme modes have, in fact, more in common with each other than either has with true vision. Unlike true vision they are forced, rigid, partial, specialized and dissociated.

Nor is true vision simply the delight of a new insight into that which has been crippling. Such an insight is like a brilliant light which dazzles until one has accommodated to it and which is valued for the very contrast to what has been before. But it is not a light by which one can live, and, only too easily, it can be idealized and those who have seen it be sanctified – a mistake which is prevalent in the counter-culture movement.

True vision which has been lost can reappear only if there is a return to the undissociated state. It is not measured or measurable, but balanced. All of oneself is put into the experience, but the experience is not isolated thereby from the rest of life. In this sense it is ordinary as opposed to special.

A Zen saying puts the matter thus :

Bankei was in the midst of a talk when the priest appeared, but the fellow made such a disturbance that Bankei stopped his discourse and asked about the noise.

'The founder of our sect,' boasted the priest, 'had such miraculous powers that he held a brush in his hand on one bank of the river, his attendant held up a paper on the other bank, and the teacher wrote the holy name of Amida through the air. Can you do such a wonderful thing?'

Bankei replied lightly : 'Perhaps your fox can perform that trick, but that is not the manner of Zen. My miracle is that when I feel hungry I eat, and when I feel thirsty I drink.'

I take this to mean that we have become so estranged from ordinary behaviour that to act in a simple way is now something of a miracle; and that specialization is, by contrast, idealized.

Because of our tendency to grade human beings as though we had a scale with which to do this, people who manifest specialized behaviour are usually regarded as either superior or inferior to the common run of mankind. The word 'normal' is used to describe those who are superior to the deviant, the word 'ordinary' to denote, in a slightly derogatory way, those who lack special gifts or training. Once a person who manifests unusual characteristics begins to think that he is a different order of being from his fellows, whether for better or worse, then his perception has become distorted and his sense of identity as a human being lessened.

Let me now turn to the practice of psychiatry in our society and consider the ways in which this profession might be afflicted with the prevailing distortions of our society.

Although certain methods may be perfectly legitimate approaches to the problems of life, there has always been a tendency to exalt a particular method into a *via regia*. In our era pride of position has been given to science, and despite the fact that the philosophical justification for the scientific explanation of the universe (logical positivism) has taken something of a beating in recent years, the impressive results of scientific endeavour in the inanimate world have ensured that its prestige remains high. Consequently, 'scientific' techniques are increasingly used in all spheres of life whether they are appropriate or not.

For a long time now medicine has been considered a branch of science and psychiatry a branch of medicine. As Sarbin puts it :

Greco-Roman medicine provided Renaissance scholars with the basic model of illness, a model that continues into the present. The patient's complaints of pains, aches, fevers, and so on, are integrated with observations of skin color, pulse, respiration, and so on, and an inference is constructed as to the probable humoral imbalance. Similarities among persons in complaints and observed signs were taken to indicate similarities or identities in the underlying etiological agent – the presence or absence of humors in certain parts of the body.

The decline of the importance of the Church in matters of unusual imaginings and conduct was parallel to the rise of science. The prestige of the scientist and his utility in filling the gap left by the withdrawal of the temporal priesthood helped in establishing the model of Galen for all kinds of illnesses – those with somatic complaints and observable somatic symptoms and those without somatic complaints but with conduct disorders substituted for somatic symptoms.[6]

The official training of the psychiatrist (that is, the doctor who specializes in the treatment of mental disorder) is still, at the present time, overwhelmingly orientated towards the organic and consists primarily in the study of the human body with special reference to the brain as a physical organ. Within this discipline – an aspect or subdivision of it – stands the practice of psychotherapy (the attempt to alleviate anguish by a psychological approach) : a speciality within a speciality within a speciality. Interest in psychotherapy has increased in recent years among the psychiatric profession, and, although in the past it has had no place in the *official* training of the psychiatrist in Britain, this will surely come as it gains in respectability; and, indeed, there are, at present, signs of a movement in this direction. But does this change overlook a fundamental dilemma?

In so far as psychiatry is primarily regarded as a branch of medicine based on the model of physical science it is the necessary and correct approach to those mechanical illnesses, such as cerebral syphilis and phenylketonuria, which manifest themselves in psychological symptoms, but is an inappropriate approach to other forms of human anguish. The present confusion of the traditional psychiatrist's role has several unfortunate consequences :

Firstly, the psychiatrist is expected to be able to understand and help personal problems in spite of the fact that his training is not necessarily concerned with these and may even decrease his chances of perceiving his patient as a person rather than a mechanism. (I refer here to his *technical* training; there is much in the non-academic, moral training of a doctor – responsibility to patients, integrity, ability to remain unnerved by crises, et cetera – which may help him in the practice of psychotherapy.)

Secondly, because of his orientation the psychiatrist will

tend not only to search for, but to be satisfied with, the demon-
stration of physiological changes in his patient : that is to say,
he is likely to assume that such changes are the cause of the
illness rather than a manifestation or complication of personal
anguish.

Thirdly, psychiatry – and the same applies to medicine –
is increasingly equipped to cure mechanical illness. But such
illness (and its treatment) involves human anguish which itself
can be confronted only by ordinary, human endeavours. Let
me give two examples of this, one a generalization not directly
concerned with illness, the other a particular case.

Mothers are nowadays encouraged to have their babies in
hospital since this has been shown to be medically safer. But
many arguments can be brought against a practice which
removes a woman from her familiar surroundings and most
intimate relationships at a time when she is, psychologically,
very vulnerable, which places her in a passive position, and
which, until very recent times, involved the removal of her
baby from her as soon as he was born. Although hospitaliza-
tion may be welcomed by some mothers it can be a harmful
experience for others, especially if their relationships with their
babies and other members of the family are unduly limited.[7]

The second example is taken from a patient of mine. She
gave me an account of her visit, a few years ago, to a mental
hospital to receive electroconvulsive treatment as an out-
patient. She had always had a dread of being 'locked up for
ever' in a mental hospital, and the sight of the bars on the
window, of patients being admitted, the sensation of being
'just a number', of not being told what was to happen, of not
seeing the psychiatrist that she had hoped to see, and so on,
added up to an experience which can only be described as
traumatic, and she cried pathetically as she recalled it.

Certain arguments could be made in defence of her
psychiatric treatment : it could have been – from a mechanical point of view – correct to give her electroconvulsive therapy
(although I do not myself believe it to have been); the
experience was traumatic to her in part because of her own

fear of madness and the fact that, like so many of the population, she had been sheltered from the experience of entering
a mental hospital; psychiatrists have an impossible burden
laid upon their shoulders – they cannot always provide personal attention to their patients or anticipate what situations
will prove traumatic. But when all this is said it remains true
that for her, as for many in a similar predicament, society
failed to treat her anguish in a human way, with the consequence that it was increased.

It becomes clear that the problem is not confined to a
particular professional discipline – psychiatry – but is a manifestation of the society in which we live. Society is unable or
unwilling to confront the plight of some of its members and
the only solution it offers at present is to place them in the
hands of specialists – and, significantly, a grossly insufficient
number of specialists – who, it is believed (either mistakenly
or cynically), have the necessary know-how, time and facilities
to cope with them.

It is undeniable that the standard of psychiatric care in our
society is abysmally poor. In their conclusion to a series of
articles on the mental health services, Donald Gould and Ann
Shearer write (*New Statesman*, 9 July 1971):

> It is important to realise that these asylums (which we now
> choose to call hospitals) were not built for the treatment of the
> mentally disabled but for their containment. They were pounds.
> It is no accident that so many of them look like prisons. Their
> history explains why there are so many of them, and why they
> come to be regarded as the proper and only place for the
> mentally abnormal, and why they have escaped involvement
> in the medical revolution which has totally changed the nature
> of every other sort of hospital.

> It explains why today they are expected to sustain their
> customers for one-fifth of the money spent on patients in a
> proper hospital.

The chief reason for this neglect of the psychiatric patient
is simply, I believe, that there is not enough love around to
provide the care for, and confront the anguish of, those who

are the most disturbed and disturbing among us. But the continued provision of such care under the auspices of traditional medicine has additional unfortunate effects : firstly, the patient with a physical, non-psychiatric disability has prior claim to the available medical resources; and secondly, the potential resources of psychiatric care which do not fit the traditional medical formula are relatively unexplored.

For reasons such as the above, one can only view the development of psychotherapy as a branch of psychiatry with misgiving, for the central dilemma of the care of psychologically disturbed people cannot be resolved by means of an impersonal, technical framework of thought. One aspect of the problem is the likely effect on the practice of psychotherapy (considered in its narrow sense as a form of psychological treatment, either individual or group) of the pervading scientific quantifying philosophy. There are already many pointers to the way psychiatry and the social 'sciences' are going : the belief that the kind of quantification which has proved so useful in physical science is appropriate to the study of persons and their problems is widespread and increasing. Although psychotherapy has as yet remained relatively free from the mechanistic and quantitative approach of 'Behaviour Therapy' (based on Pavlovian conditioning) it is in a vulnerable position. The pursuit of quantification not only leads away from an appreciation of the person as a whole[8] but ensures that a great deal of energy is expended in 'proving' rather obvious facts. Current journals and books in the field of psychiatry and psychology abound with studies which painfully reach unsurprising conclusions, such as, for example, that interpersonal stress has a bearing on psychiatric illness or that protracted separation of mother and infant is harmful to the latter – conclusions so humble that the studies make sense only if one realizes that the authors are addressing a readership deeply sceptical about the importance of personal factors in psychiatry. Such studies would seem to be less an exploratory search for truths than a translation of known truths into another idiom. It is an endeavour not unlike that of the student who forces his practical knowledge of a subject into the kind of mould which he knows (from a study of papers previously set) will satisfy the examiners.

The preoccupation with numbers is not limited to psychiatry but extends to the whole field of social science. I will take as an example a social study with implications for psychiatry – Leon Chertok's book *Motherhood and Personality: Psychosomatic Aspects of Childbirth*.[9]

Chertok, in spite of being a sophisticated observer well aware of the psychological complexities of childbirth has, I believe, been brought down by the affliction I am describing. In a study of two hundred women attending the maternity department of a Paris hospital with their first pregnancy, he attempted to identify those factors which predispose towards a successful confinement and to assess the value of 'psychoprophylactic' techniques of preparation for childbirth, applying himself to this task with a formidable thoroughness of method, involving the construction of what he calls a 'negativity grid' which charts

various traumatic and pathological occurrences, unfavourable events and circumstances, etc., which, generally speaking, might be regarded as constituting a burden of disadvantages likely . . . to have some effects on pregnancy and confinement.

And he then correlates this 'negativity' with the actual birth. The results of this mammoth endeavour are meagre. As might be expected, women with a high degree of 'negativity' tend to have more difficult births than their sisters to whom life has been kinder, and those who have been prepared for childbirth tend to do better – but not impressively better – than those who have not.

A sledgehammer has been used to crack a nut, a book promising to tell us about childbirth has lost us in a huge and sticky web of methodology, mother and baby have disappeared right in front of our eyes. One cannot dismiss the endeavour, for surely it is important to measure, in so far as this is possible, the factors predisposing to successful childbirth and to know whether psychoprophylaxis works. The fault lies, I think, not only in a failure to recognize the limitation of the quantitative approach to certain areas of experience but also the idealization of methodology, and a dread of error. No one will catch out a social scientist in a naïve emotional response to his subject, but a charge of cynicism or scepticism holds no terror for him. The result, in certain areas of research, is similar to the predicament of a person whose distrust of human nature makes him unable to consummate a relationship. But sterility is not the only hazard of excessive dependence on quantification. Another is revealed when the concept of cure is explored. Traditional psychiatry follows medicine in assuming that correct treatment aims at cure, and that cure means a restoration of normal health. Normal health, in the accepted sense, can be measured : it exists when tests upon the patient show his physiological mechanisms (for example, blood count) are, within definable limits, those of the average of the population. Although there are potential problems in this approach – particularly in a population increasingly subjected to world-wide pollution capable of altering the physiology of everyone – it works reasonably well in the field of medicine. But when we come to measure psychological abnormality, the method fails, for it cannot encompass the uniqueness of human experience and behaviour. The psychiatrist falls back on a mythical average citizen created not by God or Nature but out of the identity kit of a mass of psychological tests undertaken in laboratory conditions, or – possibly even worse – he regards his own personality structure as normal and measures the patient and his cure by the degree to which he fails to match up to it.

In contrast to this a personal approach to psychiatry is based on beliefs which derive less from the system of knowledge known as science than from the ordinary assumptions made in daily living. Persons are considered to be fundamentally different from things : to have free will and responsibility. If someone enters the consulting-room he is perceived simply and irreducibly as the person that he is – John Smith – and any attempt to explain him in other terms (as, say, the product of his genes, hormones, instincts, defences, environment, etc.) will only distort, if allowed to take precedence over the appreciation of his uniqueness to us. This is how, in the main, ordinary life is conducted, and it would seem natural to extend this approach in any attempt to understand and help those people who have become disorganized and have lost the capacity to live effectively.

That one should find the need to defend this approach might perhaps seem surprising. Yet, because of the influence of contemporary 'science', knowledge derived in the ordinary way of living and relating to people is often considered to be inferior to that gained from certain specialized methods of study (for instance, statistical) aceptable to the scientist. And so, a defence has become necessary. Fortunately, I do not myself have to attempt a defence of the position philosophically, for this has already been done: a vigorous and extensive philosophical defence of the naïve viewpoint has been made. Briefly, this defence is as follows.

The opposition to excessive or misplaced rationality in philosophy has been pursued with the greatest energy and thoroughness in Central Europe. This may be – I risk, and possibly deserve, a charge of complacent insularity in saying so – because there the need for a defence was most acute. In Britain, where there is a traditional distrust of too much logic, these excesses – at least in the realm of philosophy – have perhaps been avoided. However, for whatever reason, the seminal works of this movement (which are usually referred to as 'existential' or 'phenomenological' in outlook) are by Continental thinkers – Kierkegaard, Heidegger, Husserl, for instance – and first impressed themselves on Continental psychiatry. In more recent years, however, some important contributions to this line of thought have appeared in Britain, e.g. Michael Polanyi's *Personal Knowledge* and John MacMurray's *The Form of the Personal*. The movement has many forms, some of them mutually contradictory, and one does not have to embrace all the ideas of its adherents in order to support, and gain from, the central theme, which I take to be a recognition of the limitations of the account of persons given by scientific positivism.

In *Phenomenology of Perception* Merleau-Ponty writes:

I am not the outcome or the meeting-point of numerous causal agencies which determine my bodily or psychological make-up. I cannot conceive myself as nothing but a bit of the world, a mere object of biological, psychological or sociological investigation. I cannot shut myself up within the realm of science. All my knowledge of the world, even my scientific knowledge, is gained from my own particular point of view, or from some experience of the world without which the symbols of science would be meaningless. The whole universe of science is built upon the world as directly experienced, and if we want to subject science itself to rigorous scrutiny and arrive at a precise assessment of its meaning and scope, we must begin by reawakening the basic experience of the world of which science is the second-order expression. Science has not and never will have, by its nature, the same significance qua form of being as the world which we perceive, for the simple reason that it is a rationale or explanation of that world. I am, not a 'living creature' nor even a 'man', nor again even 'a consciousness' endowed with all the characteristics which zoology, social anatomy or inductive psychology recognize in these various products of the natural or historical process – I am the absolute source, my existence does not stem from my antecedents, from my physical and social environment; instead it moves out towards them and sustains them, for I alone bring into being for myself (and therefore into being in the only sense that the word can have for me) the tradition which I elect to carry on, or the horizon whose distance from me would be abolished – since that distance is not one of its properties – if I were not there to scan it with my gaze. Scientific points of view, according to which my existence is a moment of the world's, are always both naïve and at the same time dishonest, because they take for granted, without explicitly mentioning it, the other point of view, namely that of consciousness, through which from the outset a world forms itself round me and begins to exist for me. To return to things themselves is to return to that world which precedes knowledge, of which knowledge always *speaks*, and in relation to which every scientific schematization is an abstract and derivative sign-language, as is geography in relation to the countryside in which we have learnt beforehand what a forest, a prairie or a river is.[10]

Susanne Langer, in *Mind: an Essay on Human Feeling*, makes a similar point :

To make a fetish of 'objectivity' means to assume, in the first place, that some phenomena are intrinsically objective and others intrinsically subjective so that they can be accepted or rejected accordingly; it is one of the tacit assumptions which have frustrating metaphysical implications, and lead some great biologists and pathologists to accept strange philosophical doctrines as the only possible supports for those assumptions. In the second place it means that problems of the relationships between subjective and objective factors in mental activity are removed from the psychologist's proper sphere of investigation. These relationships, and the terms that develop in conjunction with them – symbols, concepts, fantasy, religion, speculation, selfhood and morality – really present the most exciting and important topics of the science of mind, the researches toward which all animal studies are orientated as indirect or auxiliary moves. To exclude such relationships for the sake of sure and safe laboratory methods is to stifle human psychology in embryo.[11]

Langer believes that the kind of perception relevant to understanding individual people (which can be made more accurate by a sensitivity akin to that of the artist) is largely omitted from contemporary psychology :

The direct perception of artistic import, however, is not systematic and cannot be manipulated according to any rule. It is intuitive, immediate, and its deliverances are ineffable. That is why no amount of artistic perceptiveness ever leads to scientific knowledge of the reality expressed, which is the life of feeling. What it gives us is always and only an image. But without this or some other image we cannot ask questions about the empirical data with which knowledge begins, because the image enters into the objectification of the data themselves. Unless they are objectively seen and intimately known we cannot formulate scientific questions and hypotheses about them. Here, I believe, lies the weakness of our present psychological researches : we do not really grasp the data we propose to deal with, because we are trying to transfer methods of observation simply and directly from physics to psychology, without taking account of the fact that the intraorganic character of the material presents a special difficulty and does not lend itself to those methods.[11]

I am not sure to what extent the writings of philosophers such as Merleau-Ponty and Susanne Langer (among many others whose message is essentially similar) will influence a person to think this way. They are themselves indirect communications of a logical nature, not works of art nor the immediate stuff of interpersonal experience. But if they are not likely on their own to convince they may give more rigorous formulation to impressions that were imprecisely, if firmly, held already; and this is what has happened in my own case. From my experience of ordinary life and in my work as a therapist I have come to believe in this approach to personal knowledge. When I relate to John Smith as a person and not as an abstraction (a member of a class, such as a lawyer, a Jew, a child, a case, et cetera) I learn to understand him better, I have a better chance of grasping the core of his being, and the relationship is enriching. When I fail to do this it is superficial or destructive. And the same applies to my own feeling of being understood by others. This is so rooted in my direct experience that I cannot imagine ever seriously doubting it, but theoretical writings have encouraged me to support this view and so have clarified my understanding of it.

What is the bearing of this on the practice of medicine and psychiatry? How does it affect the approach to the patient? This rather depends on the nature of his problem. If I have the misfortune to get knocked down by a lorry and am lying in a casualty department rapidly losing consciousness owing to bleeding from a ruptured artery, what I want is someone to operate upon me and patch me up with as much care and skill as possible. My requirement of him is that he function adequately as a surgeon – as an applied scientist – and therefore it is not necessary for me to see him or speak to him.

Should I survive, I may, if I value my life, feel enormous gratitude to him and wish to see him and thank him, but this is not necessarily central to the process of my cure. Before and after the operation I may be helped, in a personal way, by others – relatives, friends, doctors, nurses, etc. – but it is probable that such help will be auxiliary to my recovery.

In some illnesses the balance between personal and impersonal needs may be different. If I develop a psychosomatic complaint, or if, when life is unkind to me and I feel low, I succumb to an infection, I may need both technical and psychological help. At the other end of the spectrum my physical symptoms, if any, are secondary, and I need someone who will understand me.

Given needs of such varying kind, what sort of a social service would be most reasonable? The answer depends, to some extent, on the relative distribution, within the spectrum, of meaningful and mechanical elements. A survey of this would be enormously difficult, for no generally accepted criterion is in sight, and at present we perhaps can do no more than recognize that both are significant and had best be given comparable attention.

In a society more orientated to the personal than ours there would presumably be less need for specialists to be consulted about problems arising from interpersonal stress. But in the present state of affairs this need for 'expert' help in personal matters is a great one and we must establish a social service which makes such help more easily available than is the case at present. Should it be left to the client to make the first, provisional decision as to the nature of the trouble? Or should there be a receptionist whose orientation and experience suit him to distinguish between human suffering and physical illness: someone to correspond to the general practitioner in contemporary society but whose training would not be so exclusively centred on the organic? In any event the kind of approach I am describing would bring serious problems of organization; but such problems are of secondary importance to the question of the underlying philosophy of the approach to human distress. Moreover, the organizational problems of the health and social services under the present philosophy are gruesome; social work in particular tends to become paralysed by an inhibiting preoccupation with role and function. (How many papers, one wonders, have been written on 'the role of the social worker'.) With a recognition that the matter of care is primarily one of ordinary human endeavour, the importance – and idealization – of specialized training and function within the service would diminish. This could lead, in the future, to more adequate prevention of sickness or care for the mentally sick. The present situation is one which, in some ways, is likely to worsen. The tendency to increased specialization and length of training ensures the continuation of a scarcity of highly qualified and expensive practitioners (psychiatrists) whose function will become more and more concerned with organization, and practitioners of lesser status (such as social workers and nurses) whose training, while still arduous, is not considered sufficient to allow them to treat patients except possibly in certain circumstances under supervision. The system is self-perpetuating – as occurs in similar institutions, such as the University – and leads to an increasing gulf between the trained and the untrained, and a chronic shortage of supply of the former.

With the recognition that ordinary human qualities are of great importance in the practice of psychiatry, and a reduction in the largely irrelevant qualifications at present demanded of those who wish to enter this field, it seems likely that considerably more people would be attracted towards it. This does not mean that subsequent training of such people is unnecessary but it would be a training of a quite different nature to that undertaken at present and one in which academic qualifications would not necessarily play any part. Nor does it mean that the pursuit of biochemical research into, and treatment of, the mechanical elements of psychiatric illness would be restricted thereby; but such activity would be confined to those who had elected to work in this highly specialized area of study.

What, then, of that 'speciality' known as psychotherapy? What place would it have in such a programme? Psychotherapy – the word normally used to describe a personal approach to the patient – tends to convey a treatment, taking place in a consulting-room, in which the therapist verbally analyses the 'free associations' and dreams of the patient, in the manner of Freud. Sometimes the term psychotherapy is used to contrast the treatment being administered with that of 'full' psychoanalysis, with the implication that the former is a superficial, lightweight and relatively unskilled and unworthy version of the real thing. Not only does the latter usage bring the practice of psychotherapy into disrepute by branding it as an inferior business, but both uses of the term are far too narrow to encompass the attempt to approach the patient's problems in a way that is directly meaningful to him.

If, taking up the personal point of view of mental illness, one believes that the patient's predicament is best formulated as a disturbance of the ordinary business of living and relating to people – as a disruption of his meaningful appreciation of and capacity to deal with life – what conclusions are to be drawn as to treatment? It would seem that the most appropriate and useful way towards him is itself one that is based on the principles and experience of ordinary living – that psychotherapy is better conceptualized as a form and extension of our ordinary relationship to a distressed person rather than a specialized type of scientific discipline.

The ordinary, natural response to a disturbed person – provided that his behaviour is not too frightening and that there are no particular reasons for antagonism towards him – is a spontaneous gesture of help. We would approach him, talk to him, perhaps put an arm round him, ask him what was the matter, and in general, try to understand, encourage and befriend him. We would not classify him nor take up an attitude of dispassionate scientific interest. This natural, instinctive move – the prototype of which is, perhaps, the parent's response to a frightened child – would seem to be the one most likely to help the person and to stand as a model for psychotherapy.

What, then, is a psychotherapist? Is he simply a person who undertakes, or is allotted, the task of helping distressed people, having only those God-given characteristics possessed by the man-in-the-street to help him? Although, in my more cynical moments, I sometimes think that he is, this is not really so. With experience of, and studious dedication to, this task he becomes a bit of an expert, he acquires the ability to perceive, and respond to, the needs of the sick person better than most. If, however, he comes to believe in, and puts his trust in his expertise, as though it were a thing apart from, rather than an extension of, his natural response to the patient's distress, he may lose more than he has gained from his experience. Yet this is the danger to which a potential psychotherapist is exposed by a scientific/technical training.

An extension of the skills – if that is the right word – with which a person is ordinarily helped would involve a number of possible factors, some of which would be qualitatively no different from those capacities required in all interpersonal relationships (mother, lover, leader, etc.) but others of which would relate specifically to the needs of a psychologically sick person. Because sickness takes such varied forms and is often concealed, it is not possible to make a brief, cogent and inclusive statement about the requirements of a sick person. Instead of this I suggest that he needs a justifiable hope that help is possible, that his anguish can be understood, that he is worth helping and that life is worth living. To meet this need the therapist must respond as a person; and – since a pretence is unlikely to carry conviction – he must value the patient and believe in his potentialities. The ability to fulfil this function appears to depend less on technical knowledge than on the possession of those attitudes – such as love, concern, interest, respect, sincerity – which we describe as 'human' and which are possessed, in varying degree, by all of us. A fruitful psychotherapeutic set-up, therefore, is likely to be one in which the therapist is capable of these attitudes (not necessarily to an unusual degree) and the conditions are such as to foster them (for example, he must have a degree of freedom and security, and should, if it can be avoided, not try to treat a patient who, for some reason, appears hateful or repulsive to him).

Although writings on psychotherapeutic techniques often contain the recognition that a mutual acceptance of each other's humanness is important, they seldom explore the matter further, and focus almost exclusively on techniques of handling and interpretation, as though one can take the former recognition for granted. This puts things the wrong way round.

I shall now turn to Freud and consider his answer to the problem of human suffering; in particular, the degree to which he was successful in bridging the gap between scientific detachment and personal involvement.

4
The Merits and Limitations of Freudian Psychoanalysis

And so Adam went to bed comforted, having woven for himself an ingenious web of probabilities – the surest screen a wise man can place between himself and the truth.
GEORGE ELIOT, *Adam Bede*

Freud, more than any other, initiated and gave shape to modern psychotherapy in the West. For that reason alone we have to come to terms with him. Because he was a genius, and because, as an explorer, he was first in the field, much of what he had to say still holds good and we ignore it to our loss. I shall, therefore, set down, very briefly, those of his views that I believe to be among the most valuable.

It is a fact that areas of experience normally inaccessible to a person can be partially recaptured by means of drugs, hypnotism or other techniques which provoke a radical change of consciousness. In the late nineteenth century in Europe the method of choice was hypnotism. Psychoanalysis grew out of hypnotism but placed the patient in a position of greater responsibility. He was required, while in a conscious state, to talk openly and without reservations and to consider the meaning of these 'free associations'. He was no longer a thing from which, by means of hypnotic technique, secrets could be extracted, but a person who tried, with the help of the psychoanalyst, to make discoveries himself. He was not expected to respond passively to the admonitions of an authoritarian hypnotist ('From now on you will not be afraid of heights'), but to take charge of his own life and his own neurosis. Thus Freud retained a method of exploring unconscious experience – of enlarging the field of awareness – but in so doing did not place the patient in a passive position to the same degree. This increased the chances of unfamiliar and unwanted experiences (including those which are commonly considered to be 'symptoms') becoming acceptable, and diminished the likelihood of a loss of self-respect in being a patient. It was a technique which, in spite of seeming strange and mysterious to his generation, was nearer to ordinary discourse than that which it superseded. It enabled two people, unencumbered by previous personal entanglements, to meet each other to discuss the intimate problems of one of them in a setting given respectability by science and medicine and lacking the moralistic overtones of a religious confession.

Freud noted the reluctance with which these new areas of experience were confronted, and traced out the ingenious manœuvres adopted by people to avoid them. In so doing he showed – more comprehensively than had ever been achieved before – the ways in which perception is distorted by wish.

The most telling of Freud's observations about the psycho-analytic method of exploration were those on the subject of 'transference' : the patient brings with him hopes, fears and expectations gathered from his early experience of people and assumes that the analyst will behave towards him in a similar manner : instead of seeing the analyst as he really is, he transfers, in a rigid and stereotyped way, the feelings and perceptions that he has had towards important figures in his past, notably his parents. For instance, a person who has been an unwanted child may assume, without any evidence to support his belief, that the analyst wants to see the back of him. By carefully observing these unwarranted and unrealistic assumptions the analyst is able to call attention to deeply ingrained attitudes in the patient of which the latter had remained unaware – a technique which Freud called 'interpretation of the transference'.

Freud allowed his patients to reveal their illness in manageable form by giving them space, time and freedom – the psychoanalytical session – in which they could give up the attempt to appear normal, healthy, adapted and adult, without fear of evoking condemnation, disgust, retaliation or rejection. But the responsibility for what they did, said, thought and felt remained theirs. He provided what Winnicott has termed a 'medium' for change and growth.

By means of the psychoanalytic method Freud made certain discoveries (or rediscoveries) about human beings in health and sickness which, to my mind, still retain their validity and relevance :

Firstly, childhood – particularly early childhood – leaves its mark upon the psyche to a far greater degree than is commonly recognized, and has therefore to be explored in an attempt to understand adult illness.

Secondly, people are physical; they have bodies. The attempt to avoid recognition of this elemental fact is widespread in individuals and ideologies, and leads to psychological mutilation.

Thirdly, love (or, to depict Freud's view more accurately, physical desire) and hate are wild passions, of ruthless, cataclysmic ferocity, capable of devouring lives, and often at war with each other; they cannot be repressed except at a severe cost. The very strength of these passions ensures that living together in families and groups will involve serious interpersonal conflict.

Fourthly, a failure to establish sexual identity is crippling (though Freud's finding is marred by his idealization of masculinity).

Fifthly, people adapt to society only with a painful loss of potential (Freud – mistakenly, I believe – saw the problem largely as the inevitable and unenviable problem of mankind rather than a failure of society, as we know it, to provide a tolerable medium for growth).

Sixthly, personal conflicts are sometimes expressed in a language – such as that of dreams – whose structure is quite distinct from the logic of conscious thought.

Seventhly, people tend to defend themselves against the harsh facts of reality by indulging in wish-fulfilling fantasies: in extreme cases they retreat into a womb-like ('narcissistic') state in which they erect a powerful psychological barrier between themselves and the outer world.

Freud looked too hard, with too much of the mind of a scientist, at simplicity. What is most open to criticism in his theory is that he regarded people in terms of the concepts of natural science: he described the working of the mind as one would account for the activity of a machine – an inappropriate model, since a machine has no experience or aspirations and cannot love. This formulation has led to the tendency, in the practice of psychotherapy, towards two errors. Firstly, to *observe* the patient as an object to be fitted into a theoretical system rather than related to as a person. Secondly, to consider him as a passive thing which reacts mechanically – attracted by pleasurable stimuli, but avoiding painful ones – rather than a being who searches for meaning and truth. I shall now discuss these two tendencies.

It is not surprising that psychoanalysts are nowadays asked to treat a significant number of the children of parents who are either analysts themselves or have been analysed. This does not, I hasten to say, mean that such children are necessarily in a worse state of mental health than the rest of the population; rather it reflects an awareness that psychoanalysis is a possible source of easing pain and unleashing growth. My own impression, gained from a number of patients whose parents had been analysed, is that these children escape many of the inhibiting factors of a less enlightened upbringing, but their actions tend to be reduced into a stereotyped formula. Their parents, either from a mistaken belief that interpretations as such are necessarily beneficial or from an attempt to reinforce the authority of their commands, seem to have used psychoanalytic insight in a way that has often been undermining. One patient even reported to me that his father, in argument, would come out with the naïve assertion: 'But I'm right in this matter; after all, I'm a psychoanalyst.'* In such cases the therapeutic requirements of the child amount to a kind of antidote – an anti-analysis or possibly a non-analysis. The following example helps to illustrate this.

A young student came to me for an analysis partly on the recommendations of his father, who had been analysed himself. The overt complaint was that this young man, who was obviously very intelligent, could not adapt to his academic course sufficiently well to learn anything. The patient showed himself to be suffering from obsessional doubt. He maintained that, since nothing could be proved, he never knew whether he had a perception or a feeling or not – and that nor did I. Since he was highly versed in philosophy, and formidably verbal, my path was not entirely smooth : I could *tell* him nothing. But certain observations could be made.

Firstly, if his intellectual position was attacked, he suffered the most intense anxiety and appeared to think that he was in danger of complete annihilation. Secondly, the position he took up was a non-Freudian one. At first sight it seemed strange that he should come for therapy at all, let alone choose a therapist he knew to be of Freudian orientation, but it became apparent that he made this choice because he felt the greatest threat to his identity had come from Freudian interpretations and he needed to confront this threat : he had come to me in the hope of facing and overcoming a trauma. Thirdly, throughout childhood his father had bombarded him with psycho-analytic interpretations, taking the intellectual ground from under his feet. In self-defence, he concentrated all his energies on developing an intellectual position in which he would feel safe from these interpretations. Unable, because of his father's reductionism, to believe in his own natural perceptions, he had to construct a theory of existence which by-passed the

* Freud cannot, of course, be held responsible for the more absurd behaviour of some of his followers. But, because I am writing a critique of contemporary psychotherapy rather than a history, the degree to which current psychoanalytic thought and practice accurately represent Freud is not central to my theme.

need for such perceptions. He was unable to say to me: 'I think you are wrong: I don't *feel* such-and-such'; he could only argue with me from a detached philosophical standpoint.

The patient's obsessionality would be thought of, in Freudian theory, as a defence against physical and aggressive urges. And this interpretation would be correct in so far as it went. But another reason for his detachment from his *physical* urges was the fact that he had been compelled to resort to excessive dependence on mental (philosophical) growth; and direct, purposeful aggression (whether verbal or non-verbal) had proved fruitless against the confusing tactics of his father and therefore had been discarded in favour of a very subtle and indirect strategy which took philosophical doubt as its main weapon and was conducted at enormous cost to his potential.

I am not suggesting that Freudian interpretations are the only means by which parents diminish a child's sense of his worth and engender confusion and monotony by putting his behaviour into some kind of stereotyped abstract framework. But this example serves as a reminder of the widespread phenomenon by which a process of treatment can all too often contribute, in a new way, to the disease it is attempting to cure.

Another patient who had been watched anxiously in childhood found her sessions with me painful and embarrassing. She could not bear me to take up the – psychological – position of watcher. To be watched implied that she was, in some way, no good – a source of disappointment and worry. In order to escape my watchfulness, she had to 'get ahead of me'. At first I thought this stemmed from competitiveness, and only later did I come to recognize that her wish to evade my apprehension derived from her need to be unobservable. This need provoked a 'negative therapeutic reaction', for she had to prove that interpretations based on attentive observation were fruitless. What was required – what she forced me to do – was to relate to her in a less watchful way, to abandon the traditional psychoanalytic approach and allow her to *be*.

It might be argued that in such a case all that is necessary is to interpret the fear of being watched. Not only does this (at least, in my own experience) fail to help, but one should not really expect it to help. Such an interpretation does not acknowledge the inhibiting effect on growth (whether in child-hood or in therapy) which continuous watchfulness may exert. If the therapist continues thereafter to watch as zealously as before, the patient will realize that he does not fully believe in the interpretation himself and it will fail to convince.

This patient was able to make explicit a need which I believe is widespread among patients who come for therapy – a need to express themselves in the presence of someone who is interested in them as people, but not unduly watchful or anxious, who does not, either to satisfy his own therapeutic drive or scientific curiosity, need to understand everything about them, but who can be turned to when necessary for interpretative advice. It is ironic that the very strength of Freud's approach to patients – his attempt to see below the surface – was also its weakness, and has encouraged the kind of dehumanizing attitude which so limits the efficacy of con-temporary psychotherapy. In subjecting the other person to persistent scrutiny, the therapist not only distances himself, becoming a mere objective observer of phenomena, but fails to give to the other sufficient freedom to be and to grow.

Freud discovered – or rediscovered – areas of experience which contemporary society had repressed, but, having found them, he placed them in an intellectual setting. It is not merely that he used a mechanical, biophysical theory with which to describe people, but that he reacted to them with the intel-lectual part of himself. He brought them to order in a system of thought which is breath-taking in its scope, but dangerous in its consequences. In making a most telling attack on the 'dissociation of sensibility' – severance between thought and feeling – of which T. S. Eliot speaks in *The Metaphysical Poets* (1921), he introduced a technique for maintaining this dis-sociation. Psychoanalysts have become increasingly cognizant of the fact that intellectual awareness does not make a whole man, but they have not yet recognized that the only remedy is to de-intellectualize the process of therapy – to abandon the idea that it is a technique, an undertaking which can be successfully managed in emotional detachment.

The central position of the concept of 'defence' (the avoidance of painful truth) in Freudian psychotherapy derives from Freud's belief, to which I have referred above, that a person – particularly a child – is primarily motivated by an instinctual urge to seek pleasure and avoid pain. Schachtel makes the following criticism of this viewpoint :

Freud saw the ontogenetic beginnings of man as dominated completely by the pleasure principle, and his concept of this principle is such that it represents essentially a flight from a fight against life and reality; it is the quest to return to a state without stimulation, excitation, tension and striving. This principle, in spite of some later modifications and doubts, remained a crucial concept throughout Freud's thinking. Whether he conceived of it because he was impressed with the newborn's predominant wish to return to sleep and his first predominantly negative reactions to the impingeing stimuli of reaction, or by the wish of so many mentally disturbed people to withdraw from life and reality, or whether his view of sexual activity as primarily a discharge of tension led him to his negative concept of pleasure as a ceasing or decrease of excitation, and whether all these views, in turn, resulted from some deep running source in his own life, we do not know. In any case, he assumed that only the necessity to come to terms with reality and the wish to retain or gain the love of the parents caused the infant, gradually and reluctantly, to relinquish or control the at first all powerful striving for return to a tensionless state, perhaps for return to the womb. In order to bring about this compromise with reality the ego is formed, as a later offshoot of the id.[1]

It is true of course that we do not know whether Freud's view stemmed from a 'deep running source in his own life' – not that, if it did, the view would necessarily be invalidated by this fact – but it would appear to be one aspect of the generally low opinion of human nature held by a man who (as he confessed in a letter to Arnold Zweig) maintained a 'wholly unscientific belief that mankind on the average and taken by and large are a wretched lot'.

Freud's failure fully to appreciate the infant's natural attempt to confront life, and his consequent overvaluation of the importance of defence, caused him to underestimate the degree to which patients in therapy are, in however distorted a way, searching for truth. Furthermore, it led him to neglect the unhealthy and unnatural factors in any actual child's particular circumstance. If one believes that the universal hazards of life – such as weaning, sibling rivalry and the oedipal situation – are in themselves sufficient to make us ill, then the actual details of the particular environment in which we happen to grow – the unrealistic assumptions about the correct method of child-rearing, such as a four-hourly infant feeding, peculiar to a particular society, or depressions in the child's mother or father – are not necessarily crucial. It is, in his view, our defences which are interesting and need more exploration and what we are avoiding by means of our defences is the truth, both in so far as it is actually happening (or happened in the past) and as an inevitable fact of life, common to mankind, which we should be able to accept. This conception, therefore, leaves out of account not only the degree to which the trauma or traumas – the precipitating factor(s) of our distress – may be an unnatural occurrence to which we cannot hope to make an adequate adaptation, but the degree to which we are disturbed because the truth is not presented to us in a meaningful way – the degree to which we are confused. A trauma is both painful and confusing, and whether, in formulating our ideas about the child's reaction to trauma and in selecting for study those experiences we expect to be harmful, we stress one or the other of these two aspects, depends on our preconceptions. Freud focused on experiences that are painful and the child's wish to avoid them, to the exclusion of experiences that are confusing and the child's wish to make sense of them. To put it another way : Freud saw the child's psychopathology negatively in terms of a shrinking

c

away from the truth rather than positively as a (necessarily tortuous) search for the truth in difficult circumstances. To counteract Freud's bias we must, firstly, look for the child's – and the adult patient's – hopeful and realistic aims in his apparent defensive and passive behaviour and, secondly, explore those areas of his environment which are likely to be unduly confusing to him. (I shall return to this theme in Chapter 7.)

Up to this point I have been concerned with Freud and the main psychoanalytic tradition which has followed in his footsteps. But what of developments within the psychoanalytic movement? To what extent have the above criticisms been met? The most significant work in this area is, to my mind, that of Erik Erikson in America, that associated with the names of Melanie Klein, W. R. D. Fairbairn and Harry Guntrip in England and usually referred to by the unhappy name of 'object-relations theory', and that of D. W. Winnicott.

Erikson's concept of 'identity' has emerged with sufficient power to impress itself upon the whole intellectual scene, linking several disciplines and disturbing sterile patterns of thought. To him it implied 'both a persistent sameness (self-sameness) and a persistent sharing of some kind of essential character with others', and his extraordinarily imaginative and clinically astute writings on the subject have provided more understanding of the interaction between individual and society than those of any other thinker in recent times. The concept of identity helped psychoanalysis to come to terms with the fact that people are whole, unique beings and cannot be satisfactorily explained in terms of id, ego and super-ego. In describing the vicissitudes of the sense of identity – in particular the 'identity crisis' of adolescence – Erikson introduced a new dimension in psychiatric thinking. Because of his influence, a psychiatrist is now less likely to take a gloomy and unhelpful view of antisocial, suicidal or near-psychotic tendencies in adolescence and more likely to give the unhappy youth the support and time he needs to co-ordinate his conflicting identifications and emerge intact as an adult. Erikson's writings are so warm, so positive and so fair-minded that one's criticisms of them are inhibited. But I think he tries to explain the sense of personal identity too much in terms of identification with others and with the role required by society and myth. We each have our own unique perception and experience, much of it developed in spontaneous relationships in which society roles are of secondary importance and which give us a sense of ourselves as beings transcending the social dimension. Perhaps a greater limitation to his approach lies in the fact that, like so many psychoanalysts before him, he tries – too hard – to graft new ideas on to an outdated theory. If he had recognized the need to scrap the images of force and counterforce which constitute Freud's formulation of the human personality, he would never have called his central concept by the ungainly term of 'ego-identity'. The 'ego,' as understood by psychoanalysts, is not the self : it is a mechanistic construction, and is alienated from its source of power, the 'id'. Its importance is considered to lie in the function of organizing and harmonizing 'instinctual' urges towards pleasure. One of the failings of this theory is that it does not do justice to the human need to find meaning in life, of which Erikson himself is well aware.

The main thesis of the 'object-relations' school of thought is that, contrary to the view of Freud, the child has an innate drive to seek out others : his primary aim is not, as Freud held, mere relief from the pressures of an instinctual urge towards physical gratification. It is a theory which was anticipated by the work (neglected during his lifetime) of Ian Suttie,[2] but which first took shape within the psychoanalytic movement under the influence of Melanie Klein.

In place of Freud's formulation of instinctual release, Klein laid stress on the infant's need for a loving relationship with his mother. But, in fact, she did not make as great a step in recognizing the nature of love as might appear. Elaborating on Karl Abraham's[3] observations on infantile experience, she formed a theory of normal and abnormal development based on the conflict between the infant's desire for and hate of his *fantasied* (internalized) mother, and in particular, her breast. This theory focuses to such an extent on fantasy that the real relationship between mother and child is largely omitted and love remains, as it did for Freud, primarily a narcissistic urge. Melanie Klein's ideas throw valuable light on schizoid (splitting) mechanisms in infancy and recognize the fact that true vision involves the acceptance of tragedy. But they are of less universal relevance than she believed and retain most of the faults of Freud's own system of thought, some of them to an exaggerated degree.

W. R. D. Fairbairn[4] was more successful in forming a theory of personal relationships which does justice to the fact that mother and child are two separate people and which escapes from the preoccupation with mouth and genital which so characterizes psychoanalytic thought. However, he still conceived of the relationship primarily in physical terms and failed to confront the problem of human spontaneity and decision.

Another, slightly different, form of object-relations theory is that of John Bowlby. Although he regards instinct as the source of behaviour, Bowlby[5] does not conceive it in the terms of 'drive' or 'impulse' towards certain kinds of action (such as aggression), but as an in-built organization which responds to appropriate cues in the environment at various stages of development. Feedback mechanisms ensure that adaptation is accurate and flexible. Drawing on the work of Lorenz and other ethologists, he shows how well 'behavioural systems' can be used to explain the activity of the human infant, and gives a detailed account, in these terms, of the infant's tendency to attach himself to his mother.

The ethological position is, to my mind, at least as mechanical as the theory that it seeks to replace: the person is a programmed computer designed to propagate the species, the actual experience of life is of secondary importance; free will is out. Such philosophy will not sustain the psychotherapist and his patient. People – except some very sick ones – believe that they have free will. It is perhaps true to say that the degree to which they lack this belief is a measure of their illness. In other words, what is crucial to people – and what must form the basis of psychology and psychotherapy – is whatever involves their freedom of choice, not that which lies outside it, although the latter must be known. Bowlby has charted areas (which we share with animals) lying beyond the realm of decision – such as, for instance, the automatic smiling response of the infant to a human face or a mask resembling a face – but this theory, in so far as he has formulated it up to the present, does not encompass the most significant areas of experience.

Finally, I come to D. W. Winnicott, who is, perhaps, the most creative thinker in the field of psychotherapy – whether inside or outside the psychoanalytical movement – since Freud. In common with others I have mentioned in this chapter, Winnicott describes the child's urge to form personal relationships rather than his need to release instinctual tension. In nearly all of his writings, one gets the impression that he is thinking about the child as a person who seeks out his own destiny – who is concerned with the meaning of life, and who, even when acting defensively, is making choices rather than responding automatically as a mechanism.

Perhaps the most valuable of Winnicott's contributions to psychotherapy is his conception of a 'true self', which can remain intact, though hidden, during infancy, awaiting the possibility that in later years circumstances may permit it to emerge. During this period of concealment, it is protected by a 'false self', which makes an apparently successful adaptation to society. The task of the therapist, in this event, is to engender sufficient trust in the patient for him to abandon his 'false self', and then to 'hold' him during the subsequent period of confusion while the 'true self' is developing.

Like Erikson, Winnicott does not confront the fact that his own theories cannot be left to live side by side with those of Freud, as though they were simply compatible. For instance, of his own formulation of early child development, he writes :

The theory relative to this important stage in ontogenetic development belongs to the observation of infant-to-mother (regressed patient-to-analyst) living, and it does not belong to the theory of early mechanism of ego-defence organised against id-impulse, though of course, these two subjects overlap.[6]

The chief defect of Winnicott's work is that he identifies the psychotherapeutic encounter too closely with mothering – and romanticizes both experiences. This leads to a relative neglect of two factors : firstly, the importance of the father, and, secondly, the way in which the concept of therapeutic regression (the state in which the patient feels like a baby in the presence of a mother) can be abused for parasitic or aggressive purposes (to put it another way : Winnicott's writings at times involve an idealization of the state of regression). These two omissions are, I think, related, in that one traditional function of the father is to help his children towards a place outside the shelter and safety of the home.

Because my own thinking has been greatly influenced by Winnicott's writings on the emergence of the true self during the course of psychotherapy, I shall refer to his ideas on the subject on several occasions later in the book.

The line of argument pursued in this chapter suggests that Freud did not succeed in emancipating himself from the scientific philosophy of his time, and that contemporary psychoanalysis, although it has made further advances in the direction of a more human theory of personal relationships – and contains, within the movement, some very creative and fruitful thinkers – has also failed to free itself entirely from a mechanistic view of personal life and the psychotherapeutic experience. I shall now discuss another movement – the existential–phenomenological approach – which specifically sets out to transcend the scientific attitude to human beings.

5
The Existential – Phenomenological Approach to Psychotherapy

But let there be no scales to weigh your
unknown treasure;
And seek not the depths of your knowledge
with staff or sounding line.
For self is a sea boundless and measureless.
KAHLIL GIBRAN, *The Prophet*

The 'existential' or 'phenomenological' school of thought, to which I drew attention in Chapter 3, constitutes a more appropriate philosophy of man than that of scientific rationality. It regards the person as a unique, spontaneous being who cannot be adequately described in those terms which have proved useful in our assessment of the inanimate world, and it lays stress on the importance of viewing phenomena in a simple and direct way that is not disturbed by a preoccupation with underlying causes. In the context of psychiatry this means that the important question is *what* the patient is experiencing; *why* he experiences things as he does is secondary; the aim is to find one's way into the perceptual world of the patient, to see things as he sees them, rather than explain his behaviour in terms which have been brought in from outside his experience – such as 'case-history' or 'environment' – and which are therefore inappropriate.

The major philosophical figures in the existential-phenomenological movement – Hegel, Kierkegaard, Husserl,

Heidegger, Sartre and Merleau-Ponty – and the psychiatrists who developed this kind of approach in their clinical work – notably Minkowski and Binswanger – were of European origin. This movement has had an increasing influence on psychotherapy, but it has no well-defined membership. It does not, like Freudian psychoanalysis, derive its main inspiration from the work of one man, and it is often impossible and would anyway perhaps be fruitless to decide whether a certain psychiatrist is an 'Existentialist' or not. (Because I have written about psychotherapy in an 'existential' way I am sometimes asked if I will give an 'existential analysis' but it is a question to which I can find no useful answer.) In writing about the movement, therefore, I am less concerned to give it an exact formulation or identify its adherents than to discuss ideas emerging from this ill-defined area of thought which seem to me most relevant to the theme of this book, and to which I have felt myself responsive. The movement has taken a rather different form in Britain from that in America, largely, I think, because the influence of Sartre has been much greater in the former country.

Sartre, like Freud, is a pessimist. He takes the view that 'all existing beings are born for no reason, continue through weakness and die by accident'. Life, for him, is an absurd and irrational occurrence; the only proper response to it is 'nausea'; to accept it, as does the ordinary man, is to act in 'bad faith'; love is not possible and the best one can aim for in society is the manipulation of those who are trying to manipulate oneself. A reading of Sartre's autobiography, *Words*, suggests that he has made the common mistake of assuming that the peculiar experiences of his own unhappy childhood were universal and formulating a general system of philosophy and psychology on their basis.

But Sartre's pessimism takes a different form from that of Freud. To Freud the dilemma is that the child is by nature wilful and greedy and must be painfully coerced into accepting the superior rationality of others; to Sartre it lies in the simple impossibility of the child's needs being met by others in any meaningful way. Whereas Freud says, in effect, 'It's a bloody life, but accept it', Sartre says 'It's a bloody life; reject it.' Both of them take sides in a dialogue which cannot be solved by taking sides but neither believes that the gulf between self and other can be bridged. They both fail, I think, to make a distinction between the anguish and tragedy that is the common lot of mankind and the alienation experienced by those children whose parents are unable to give them a sense that they have a place in this world. The difference is crucial.

To deny the tragic facts of existence and to refuse to accept the inevitable hardships and limitations of the world is to escape into wish-fulfilling fantasy and live a false and super-ficial life. But the arbitrary, unnecessary and even savage curtailments which a particular society or family may impose upon a child present a problem which must be accepted as existing yet resisted as something which should not be there. The predicament of the child is to understand which of these two kinds of restriction – the inevitable or the arbitrary – is facing him, and to take appropriate action. Ironically the over-protected child has the worst of both worlds : he is not given the sense that he could and should withstand the real rigours of living, yet he is subjected to pressures which are peculiar to the style of his particular upbringing. For instance, a child has to learn the implacable fact that he cannot be in two places at one and the same time, but he should not have to 'learn' such false theories as that if he masturbates he will do himself incalculable harm. This is a subject to which I shall return in Chapter 8, as it has significant bearing on the psychotherapeutic encounter, raising such questions as : 'To what extent is the traditional psychotherapeutic set-up a necessary or an arbitrary creation? If the patient resists the assumptions of the therapist as to how the relationship should be, is he turning away from reality or making a justified criticism of an alienating procedure?'

*

The three British psychiatrists whose writings have been most influenced by Sartre are R. D. Laing, Aaron Esterson and David Cooper, and the two most important of their books are Laing's *The Divided Self* and a joint work by Laing and Esterson, *Sanity, Madness and the Family*. I have discussed these works elsewhere[1] and shall refer again to the second one in Chapter 6.

The Divided Self was a breath of fresh air. In it, Laing described, in terms which conveyed the actual experience, the predicament of those people, usually called 'schizoid' or 'schizophrenic', who have withdrawn in despair from a world in which they appear to have no place. It constituted a (largely implicit) criticism of a society which permitted this to happen and which prevented any possibility of real treatment by labelling those unfortunate people 'sick' or 'abnormal'. *Sanity, Madness and the Family*, an account of a research project, which draws not only on the philosophy of Sartre but also on recent American studies of families in which an offspring is labelled 'schizophrenic', continues the argument, focusing on an indictment of a family system which, in some cases, can psychologically crush its children. The condemnation of society, and in particular, its treatment of children and the mentally sick, gathers steam in Laing's *The Politics of Experience and The Bird of Paradise* and reaches its ultimate – in dogmatism and absurdity – in David Cooper's two books *Psychiatry and Anti-Psychiatry* and *The Death of the Family*. Cooper lacks Laing's coherence of expression, and his recent critique of the contemporary family (*The Death of the Family*) is spoiled by grossly overstating a valid argument. Even his least confused statements omit a whole area of reality. For instance, he writes:

Take a very ordinary situation between parent and child. Parent walks down the high street holding his child's hand. At a certain point there is a necessary breakdown of reciprocity – the parent holds the child's hand but the child no longer holds the parent's hand. By a subtle kinesic alteration in hand pressure, the child of three or four years indicates to the parent that she wants to make her own way down the high street in her own time. The parent either tightens his grip or takes what he has been taught to experience as a fearful risk – to let his child leave him not in his time or in socially prescribed time but in the child's time.[2]

There is no indication here that Cooper is aware that – as statistics and experimental tests have shown – it is indeed a 'fearful risk' for a child to have freedom in the high street in the era of the motor car. This is but one example of Cooper's assumption that parents' care of their children is entirely based on an unnecessary and possessive infringement of their rights; parental love does not, for him, exist.

It would be a sad thing if the extremism of some of this later writing impaired our reception of the important insights of the early work. Laing uses Sartre's pessimism creatively in writing vividly of the alienated state and identifying some of the factors which lead a person to this condition of mind. But his pessimism is also his limitation. Laing's indictment of present society, like Sartre's indictment of life, is too sweeping. In my view he underestimates the presence of love and hope which exists even in destructive and confusing families, and consequently does not lay stress – as does Winnicott – on the possibility of therapeutic help if a person can trust another and allow himself to become dependent. As David Holbrook puts it : Laing

cannot emphasise growth in relational therapy; nor can he see any hope in 'contributing in' to the family and social order. The 'rebirth' he offers is an extra-personal, cosmic affair; it is, above all, not 'weak', in the recognition that we may after all be no more than human.[3]

It is a paradoxical fact that so many attempts to bridge the gap between the powerful and the weak become corrupted in the very process they are opposing. Laing tried to show that patients and psychiatrists are equal beings, and demonstrated that the patient's viewpoint is more valid than had been hitherto suspected, but he ended by exaggerating the impasse. This was due in part I think to his failure to recognize that people are equal and ordinary. The schizophrenic, for him, is no ordinary person, but a superior being; society, in his view, does not consist of ordinary people who, in a rather haphazard and messy way, love and hate, adapt or revolt, succeed or fail, but a system organized towards certain (destructive) ends; and, for him, inevitably, psychotherapy is not an ordinary business.

The existential–phenomenological approach in America has taken a form which, if less arresting and exciting than the British version, is more optimistic in outlook. Prominent writers in this field – such as Victor Frankl, Abraham Maslow and Rollo May – write with clarity on the principles involved in 'meeting' or 'encountering' the patient as a fellow human being rather than an object of study, and seeking to evoke the creative possibilities within him. Thus Rollo May writes :

Our chief concern in therapy is with the potentiality of the human being. The goal of therapy is to help the patient actualize his potentialities. The joy of the process of actualizing becomes more important than the pleasure of discharged energy – though that itself, in its own context, obviously has pleasurable aspects, too. The goal of therapy is not the absence of anxiety, but rather the changing of neurotic anxiety into normal anxiety, and the development of the capacity to live with and use normal anxiety. The patient after therapy may well bear more anxiety than he had before, but it will be conscious anxiety and he will be able to use it constructively. Nor is the goal the absence of guilt feeling, but rather the transformation of neurotic guilt into normal guilt, together with the development of the capacity to use this normal guilt creatively.[4]

But despite the urgency of its desire to avoid the mistake which the scientist makes, in reducing the reality of the encounter between therapist and patient into abstract terms, this genre of writing uncannily tends to fall into the same (or a very similar) error : discussions not seldom lack cogency because of ponderous philosophical arguments or woolly platitudes. Rollo May himself is well aware of the dangers of the latter and writes of the tendency to use such terms as 'transcendence', 'encounter', 'presence' as a way of bypassing existential reality. We hear in discussions and papers, for example, such references to the 'transcendence' assumedly occurring in psychotherapy as 'transcendence of the subject–object dichotomy between therapist and patient', 'transcendence of the body–mind dichotomy', 'transcendence of dualistic thought', 'transcendence of the epistemic barrier between man and Ultimate Reality (God)'. The term 'encounter' is used – or rather misused – with a kind of halo to varnish over the very difficult problems of interpersonal relationships and their distortion, and the term 'presence' is misused to cover up the fact that understanding another person genuinely is a very difficult process in the best of situations and is never possible in a complete sense.[4]

But, since the best of this school of writing is very good and constitutes an outlook which I believe to be right, I have wondered why I do not emotionally respond to it as much as I would expect. The conclusion I have reached is that the creativity of this school has become restricted by a preoccupation with the definition of the therapeutic process. The problem in writing about psychotherapy – a problem which at times leads me to despair over writing this book – is to prevent words and concepts from getting between oneself and the actual life-situation. Whereas the danger to the scientist is to fragment and compartmentalize life, the Existentialist tends towards an obsessional urge to exactitude in defining the total experience. If, on the other hand, one were to accept the limitations of concepts, one might be more content to describe, in a rough and ready way, the particularities of therapeutic experience which seem to be the most meaningful. Some of the most creative writers in the field of psychotherapy – such as Harold Searles – do, I believe, work in this manner, recognizing that, since a perfect map is unavailable, they have to hack their way through the thistles, using whatever imperfect tools are to hand.

There is an additional reason, I think, for the relative failure of Existential Psychotherapy to make as creative an advance as one might have expected : the departure from Freud's basic insight into the necessity of returning to the past in therapy – in other words the recognition that we are all children – has been too radical. I will discuss this further in the next chapter. In the meantime I want to refer to the work of another American, Carl Rogers. Carl Rogers regards himself as a psychotherapist who works within the existential tradition, but his interest lies less in the general philosophy of this move- ment than in the actual details of psychotherapeutic procedure. No one has studied what passes between therapist and patient more thoroughly and systematically than he, and his methods and findings have been very influential, particularly in America; indeed there exists a 'Rogerian' approach to treatment.

Rogers calls his method 'client-centred' or 'non-directive' therapy. If a therapist is to be successful Rogers believes he must abandon all attempts to formulate the client in diagnostic categories, and instead must simply try to understand the pre- dicament as the client himself sees it; in so doing he implicitly encourages the client to believe in his own capacity to solve his problems and, by respecting him as he is, enables him to feel a greater self-respect. Rogers is insistent that the respect felt by the therapist must be genuine – a pretence will soon be seen through. Let Rogers speak for himself :

In the emotional warmth of the relationship with the therapist, the client begins to experience a feeling of safety as he finds that whatever attitude he expresses is understood in almost the same way that he perceives it, and is accepted. He then is able to explore, for example, a vague feeling of guiltiness which he has experienced. In this safe relationship he can perceive for the first time the hostile meaning and purpose of certain aspects of his behaviour, and he can understand why he has felt guilty about it, and why it has been necessary to deny to awareness the meaning of this behaviour. But this clearer perception is in itself disrupting and anxiety-creating, not therapeutic. It is evidence to the client that there are disturbing inconsistencies in himself, that he is not what he thinks he is. But as he voices his new perceptions and their attendant anxieties, he finds that this acceptant alter ego, the therapist, this other person who is only partly another person, perceives these experiences too, but with a new quality. The therapist perceives the client's self as the client has known it, and accepts it; he perceives the contradictory aspects which have been denied to awareness and accepts those too as being a part of the client, and both of these acceptances have in them the same warmth and respect. Thus it is that the client, experiencing in another an acceptance of both these aspects of himself, can take toward himself the same attitude. He finds that he too can accept himself even with the additions and alterations that are necessitated by these new perceptions of himself as hostile. He can experience himself as a person having hostile as well as other types of feelings, and can experience himself in this way without guilt. He has been enabled to do this (if our theory is correct) because another person has been able to adopt his frame of reference, to perceive with him, yet to perceive with acceptance and respect.[5]

I do not think there is any writer who has spelled out this truth of psychotherapy so thoroughly as Rogers : what is essential in treatment is that a relationship grows in which the client can risk revealing himself as a knave and a fool because he trusts that the therapist will respect him even when he cannot respect himself.

It is not a question of an all-knowing and learned therapist making correct interpretations about a patient's behaviour; rather the therapist provides a human setting in which the patient feels safe enough to explore himself. This short account does not do justice to the care and thoughtfulness with which Rogers presents his views and confronts the problems involved in such an approach. Although Rogers' influence on the psychotherapeutic scene is, I believe, a very beneficial one, I have two criticisms to make.

Firstly, Rogers gives the impression that the therapist remains calm and unemotional throughout the proceedings. Commenting on a certain patient's treatment, he writes :

How shall we understand the counselor's function as it was experienced by this client? Perhaps it would be accurate to say that the attitudes which she could express but could not accept as a part of herself became acceptable when an alternate self, the counselor, looked upon them with acceptance and *without emotion*. It was only when another self looked upon her behaviour without shame *or emotion* that she could look upon it in the same way. These attitudes were then objectified for her, and subject to control and organisation.[5] [italics mine]

This impression is increased if one considers Rogers' efforts to gain intellectual control of what happens in therapeutic encounters: his tape-recording of sessions, his immense pre-occupation with statistical findings of the results of therapy. The conclusion that I draw from this is that Rogers, despite his recognition that technical methods (such as classification into diagnostic categories) are destructive to relationships, is not himself entirely free from a need to stand back from a client and take up the posture of a mature, disciplined person who remains unruffled in the face of the patient's anxiety and anguish. While accepting that it is sometimes necessary to conceal one's own anxiety when confronted by panic, it seems to me that a consistently unemotional attitude opens up a gap between the two people: the patient is likely to feel inferior in the face of such self-control.

In the second place, Rogers gives insufficient recognition to Freud's discovery of the child in the adult; he works in the present at the expense of the past; to put it another way, he underestimates the degree to which patients transfer their childhood conflicts on to the therapeutic encounter.

As we examine our clinical experience in client-centred therapy and our recorded cases, it would appear to be correct to say that strong attitudes of a transference nature occur in a relatively small minority of cases, but that such attitudes occur in some degree in the majority of cases.

With many clients the attitudes towards the counselor are mild, and of a reality, rather than a transference, nature. Thus such a client may feel somewhat apprehensive about first meeting the counselor; may feel annoyed in early interviews that he does not receive the guidance he expected; may feel a warm rapport with the counselor as he works through his own attitudes;

leaves therapy with a gratitude to the counselor for having provided him the opportunity to work things out for himself, but not with a dependant or strong gratitude; and can meet the counselor socially or professionally during or after therapy with little affect beyond what is normally involved in the immediate reality of their relationship. This would seem to describe for many, perhaps for a majority of our clients, the affect which is directed toward the counselor. If one's definition of transference includes all affect toward others, then this is transference; if the definition being used is the transfer of infantile attitudes to a present relationship in which they are inappropriate, then very little if any transference is present.[5]

Rogers' belief that the therapist should maintain a calm and unemotional attitude towards his patient is similar to that of Freud. But the two thinkers differ widely in their view on how the patient should be expected to behave. Whereas Freud expects him to act like a child, and to transfer his childlike expectations of others on to the therapist, Rogers expects him to act as an adult who can, if given a chance, manage his own affairs. Although I have more sympathy with Rogers' approach, which carries a greater respect for the other than that of Freud, I think that both views are incorrect. Whereas Freud underestimates the adult in the patient, Rogers underestimates the child. The error, in both cases, lies in a lack of respect for the nature of the child – an idealization of the controlled type of behaviour which is traditionally accepted as adult and mature. The therapeutic encounter has much in common with that between parent and child – it is a relationship in which one person helps another to grow – and therefore the therapist will unconsciously transfer his own assumptions about adults and children on to his formulations about the nature of psychotherapy. If these assumptions constitute an exaggerated idea of the difference between child and adult (an idea characteristic of our culture), then the therapist – be he Freud or Rogers or you or I – will try to bridge a gap of his own making. If, on the other hand, he recognizes that we are all, in a sense, children, and this is not to our discredit, then he will be able not only to give full value to the regressed (childlike, emotional) behaviour of his patient, but by being vulnerable and childlike himself will enable such behaviour to emerge the better. This is a theme on which I shall dwell in subsequent chapters. In the meantime I want to consider an attempt to bridge this gap which has widespread appeal at the present time but which, in my view, is based on false premises.

In recent years a movement has emerged which had its origin on the West coast of America, notably at the Esalen Centre at Big Sur. There is, so far as I know, no single term to describe the diverse therapeutic approaches of the movement (perhaps 'Encounter Groups' is the name most frequently used), and the sources of inspiration came from many areas, including Zen Buddhism, existential philosophy, Wilhelm Reich and hallucinogenic drugs.

In the hands of Carl Rogers[6] 'Encounter Groups' emerge as traditional forms of group therapy modified by the author's personal approach discussed above, with the significant difference that the 'facilitator' (as he prefers to call the group therapist) is depicted as someone who expresses his own feelings more readily than the therapist engaged in one-to-one relationships previously described by Rogers. Our evaluation of such encounters must in part depend on our estimation of the relative potency of individual and group therapy. In my view a group, however enriching to some, cannot hope to give the focused attention over a period of time which so many disturbed people need through which to reveal the intricate problems of their childhood. Be that as it may, Rogers' thoughtful and sober writing is not characteristic of the movement as a whole.

Frederick Perls, who introduced a form of treatment known as 'Gestalt Therapy', is a key figure at Esalen. Perls conducts therapeutic groups in which he attacks, with great vigour, the conventional verbal intercourse with which people try to keep one another at a distance, and cuts through their comfortable and polite evasions by calculated rudeness. They are forced to make their contributions in unaccustomed ways –

perhaps by simply looking at one another. It is a technique rather similar to that used by William Schutz, who encourages his group to act out their conflicts and fantasies on a physical plane. The impact of Esalen comes not only from the organized seminars but from the whole tenor of living there. Most of the conventions and *mores* of ordinary society are discarded in favour of spontaneity and freedom of expression. These various modes of living and conducting therapy would seem to have a common desire to make personal contact with more emotional truth than is possible in present-day society – and perhaps in most societies of the past. A particular technique used both in the practice of Zen and the group therapy sessions described is that of shock – a shock which, unlike the electrical ones administered by psychiatry, is psychologically meaningful : the social games which enable a person to get by are dramatically exposed for what they are worth and he is suddenly confronted with the barrenness of his previous way of perceiving the world.

There is surely no fault in the endeavour. But the method is another matter. Whereas the path of salvation is notoriously painful and difficult, Encounter Groups try to get there at one stroke. Our inhibitions have been gradually constructed in meaningful and complicated personal contexts and must be resolved in a similar way. There are no short cuts – it is not enough to touch, hug, shout or have sex – and these methods are technical procedures which can in the end be no more successful than hypnosis or drug abreaction treatment. The changes which occur – in those for whom the experience is more than a playful and healthy, albeit superficial, release – are not, in my view, of the kind which occur when a deep psychological wound is healed. There is little use in taking a good solid obsessional square from Los Angeles and converting him overnight into a hysteric.

I should not, of course, label *people* 'obsessional' and 'hysteric'; there are no such beings. But the terms are descriptively valid – indeed, one of the few useful ways of describing pathological behaviour that we possess, and can, I believe, help to throw light on the phenomenon I have just described. They describe extreme forms of the two kinds of perceptual distortion, subjective and objective, that I discussed in Chapter 3 : an extreme objectivity constitutes obsessionality, whereas extreme subjectivity manifests itself as hysteria. Both are partial, distorted, one-sided views of reality, and thus they have much in common : their similarities are more important than their differences.

Of Mr Enoch Powell's activities *The Times* writes (15 June 1970) :

Yet it is ludicrous to suppose that any British Party could ever now be led by Mr Powell. The Conservative Party has many faults, but it is a very English Party, and the English, the central nation of the United Kingdom, are much more phlegmatic than hysterical. The Conservative Party, in this way much like the Labour Party, reacts away from obsession, from hysteria, from men of destiny, true or false.

One looks to *The Times* for political opinion rather than a psychiatric one, but in this case the leader writer has, I think, shown sound psychiatric sense. What is disturbing in Mr Powell's speeches is the overall absence of that spontaneous, authentic, natural flexibility which makes us feel we are listening to a man of wisdom and humanity. Whether we focus on the 'hysterical', emotive, exaggerated nature of his speeches, or on his 'obsessive' over-serious preoccupation with the same themes, is of secondary importance.

One distinction that is often made between hysteria and obsessionality is that the former is thought to signify a loss of control, the latter, excessive control. (In Freudian terminology : hysteria connotes an invasion of the controlling ego by the forces of instinct, obsessionality a preoccupation with defence against instinct.) The implication – that obsessionality is a more defensive kind of behaviour – is, I think, wrong. The two represent, in exaggerated form, ordinary and healthy modes of experience. Hysteria is a caricature of personal behaviour (more typically feminine); obsessionality of impersonal behaviour (more typically masculine). In the pathological forms of these two styles of living, certain responses to disturbing situations get out of hand. The hysteric focuses on her relationships with other people (especially men) to such an extent that she becomes incapable of impersonal action. The obsessional is so concerned with the impersonal organization of circumstances that he becomes unaware of human experience. Each, in his way, denies reality; each has lost control of himself – although the loss is only manifest in the hysteria; each has become rigid – although the rigidity is only obvious in the obsessional.

The existential–phenomenological movement came into being to oppose the obsessional preoccupation with dehumanizing concepts and explanations of man. But, as Eliot wrote,

> *every attempt*
> *Is a wholly new start, and a different kind of failure* :

our 'raid on the inarticulate/With shabby equipment' can so easily be corrupted by the very faults we are trying to combat. Existentialism fails both where it becomes preoccupied with abstruse and abstract, obsessional formulations about the nature of reality, and when, in lieu of the difficult, delicate, gradual approach to the true self of the other, it attempts in an hysterical fashion to manufacture intimacy by means of instant therapy.

Finally, I must refer to the work of the Swiss psychotherapist, Medard Boss, whose ideas are accessible to English readers in his book *Psychoanalysis and Daseinsanalysis.* The title is unfortunate, for it suggests that another school of thought is setting itself up in opposition to that of Freud. But if one can be tolerant of yet another example of the ubiquitous tendency to found sects, and if those with little taste for philosophy can survive Boss's preoccupation with the ideas of Heidegger, there is to be found here the work of a therapist who gives one the feel of the consulting-room, who, although dissatisfied with the psychoanalytic technique of transference interpretation, is deeply aware of the child in the patient : Boss comes close to the most fruitful trends in British psychoanalysis (although he is not aware of this).

He recognizes that what gives the breath of life to patients is less a verbal interpretation of their predicament than a relationship in which they can grow. Intensely critical of the psychoanalytical concept of 'acting out' (the idea that a patient repeats, in the form of action, past events as a defence against remembering and talking about these events), he writes :

The last thing our analysands need is a theoretical reduction of their acting-out to a transference phenomenon – or any other rational explanation of it. Nor do they need to account for it, intellectually (with or without the corresponding 'affects'), to reflect on it 'consciously,' to articulate it verbally, or to assume full responsibility for it. Their primary requirement is not some kind of conceptual recognition of their acting-out, but rather the opportunity to live and to experience, over and over again, immediately and unreflectingly, their new ways of behaviour within the safe relationship to the analyst.[7]

Boss emphasizes the need for a patient to be given permission to grow, and suggests that the question 'Why?' is a less useful and productive one than 'Why not?' :

The author once asked 'Why?' in an attempt to enable a patient, a thirty-five-year-old woman, to come to a quick rational understanding of her acting-out. The question was asked at the wrong time; although the worst could eventually be avoided, the question probably added two years to the analysis. What happened was as follows. The patient, after tremendous inner resistance had been overcome, got off the couch and began to kneel on the floor, leaning against the couch. When the analyst asked her why she was doing this, she interpreted his question (as is only too often the case) as a prohibition. In reality, the analyst, faithful to Freud's advice, had intended to transform her acting-out into a memory. The (supposed) meaning of this kneeling gesture was to be understood intellectually and expressed verbally. But the patient was not ready for such expression. Her condition was still comparable to that of a small child; she was still capable of expressing what she wanted to express only in the language of gestures appropriate to a small child.

This area of experience – the circumstances in which a patient may risk a second, late, attempt to unfold his true self – is, to my mind, one of the key issues of psychotherapeutic endeavour, and I shall devote the next chapter to this question.

Although I have made certain criticisms of the Existential movement, it offers, for me at least, an intellectual framework that is more appropriate to the formulation of psychotherapeutic experience than any other. Traditional scientific formulations unhappily help the therapist to preserve the illusion that he is a different order of animal from the patient, that he does not also experience the emotional torments that are inescapable for anyone who is in touch with his feelings. What is crucial, at the present time, is to understand and, where possible, report on therapeutic encounters as they actually happen when the artificial distancing between therapist and patient is abandoned.

However great the gains from an open encounter between therapist and patient one still pauses to wonder what might be lost : in particular, can the transference be clearly seen if the therapist responds spontaneously rather than holding back in order to analyse? I believe it can – and will return to this question in Chapter 8 – but let me end the present chapter with an example.

Janet had been coming to me for two years. She considered all that she did and felt in a very intellectual way, and although she was able to tell me in words about the intense feelings that she experienced during sessions she could not communicate these feelings in her way of speaking and acting. And this made a barrier between us. Although I liked her and never found the sessions wearisome I often felt a slight uneasiness in her presence. Most of all I was inhibited by her idealization of me, and found myself thinking, 'If only she knew what I was really like, how disillusioned she would be.' I wanted this disillusionment yet feared it, for her admiration gave false satisfaction to my self-esteem.

During one particular session Janet lost her usual composure. 'I'm not fit to live,' she said. 'I'm so *awful*. I'm just hopeless. I'm not fit to be here. You must feel that.'

There was something very moving in the way she said this and it found immediate echoes in my own experience. I remembered occasions, in both distant and recent times of my life, when I had known the same feeling of shame and despair in the presence of another person. And I felt a lessening of my own urge to keep up a pretence of roadworthiness in order to match Janet's idealization of me and satisfy my own impulse to bask in this.

I said, 'No, I feel quite the *opposite* of what you expect. I just feel relieved. It makes you feel human like me. Now you know what I can feel like. It makes me think you can stand *me*.'

Janet said little but I think she recognized the truth of my response and its importance to me.

In the next session Janet was still feeling very vulnerable and was cold and shivery. 'I feel as though I've got no proper shape – a bit like a cloud when there's no sharp edge to it. Do *you* ever feel like that?' She asked me again what despair felt like to me and became disturbed when I told her. I asked her why it disturbed her so much. 'I feel hurt,' she answered. 'I feel hurt because it means I'm not good enough to make you happy. If I were valuable – if I were lovable to you – you wouldn't feel despair. It means I'm no good to you.' I said that this wasn't true. For if I felt despair and she accepted it, I would feel (if only a bit) better. At this point she or I (I forget who) recalled her mother's despair and Janet's feeling of inadequacy at being unable to do anything about it.

But this interchange did not relieve Janet. In the next session she continued her idealization of me, although in a different form. 'You are more in touch with your own feelings than I am,' she said. 'It makes me feel inferior.' I began to feel that however open I might be about myself – whatever inadequacies I might demonstrate – Janet would continue to find *some* reason to whitewash me and think me superior to her. I told her this, and added that I felt that much of her feeling of inferiority was a pretence – that, in fact, she needed to brainwash me, for *my* sake, into believing that I was a great guy. Janet agreed with this interpretation. Once again, we both realized that this was a transference : that she had felt, in exactly the same way, the need to protect her mother from the latter's sense of insecurity and unhappiness.

Thus, in showing some of my feelings of inadequacy, I did not confirm her compulsive need to see me as weak and to protect me from this perception. If anything, it had the reverse effect, for it helped Janet to recognize that I did not need her to protect me from her own perception of my limitations as *much* as she imagined. Nor did it prevent the emergence of the past (the transference) and our ability to recognize it.

It is very difficult to assess the relative importance of various features in a therapeutic encounter of the kind I have described. A Freudian would, I think, place most emphasis on the transference interpretations as the effective factors in any change which took place. But I believe the moment in which Janet revealed her despair and my non-interpretative response to this to be at least as important and perhaps crucial, and it was that moment that Janet remembered vividly when I showed her this account some months after it occurred. I do not mean to suggest that this particular interchange was decisive to the analysis, that it marked an absolute turning-point, or that there was anything extraordinary in it. But I think it was one of many occurrences between us in which we saw the possibility of risking disillusionment in ourselves and each other, enabling us gradually to come closer together. And without these moments we would have got nowhere.

6

The Hopeful Return
to the Past

I've come to an end: if only someone else could begin at the point where I've ended. There are times when I have the impression that everything's in its place, ready to sing together in harmony. The machine on the point of starting. I can even imagine it in motion, alive, like something unsuspectedly new. But there's still something: an infinitesimal obstacle, a grain of sand, shrinking and shrinking and yet unable to disappear completely. I don't know what I ought to say or what I ought to do. Sometimes that obstacle seems to me like a teardrop wedged into some articulation of the orchestra, keeping it silent until it's been dissolved. And I have an unbearable feeling that all the rest of my life won't be sufficient to dissolve this drop in my soul. And I'm haunted by the thought that, if they were to burn me alive, this obstinate moment would be the last to surrender.

GEORGE SEFERIS, *Mr Stratis Thalassinos Describes a Man*

It is, as Freud showed, crucial to our understanding of mental ill health to recognize that we are what we have grown out of : when confusions and terrors afflict us which cannot be accounted for in our present life they have come to us from the past. Thus, in psychotherapy, much of what happens is inevitably concerned with what went wrong in childhood. I do not mean that the patient necessarily gives an account of his childhood in words but that, in bringing himself, he cannot but help include those aspects of childhood experience which have left their hurt. He may, for instance, expect that the therapist will spoil him because his parents spoilt him. In Freud's terms he 'transfers' his early ideas about other people on to the therapist.

To a certain extent this repetition of past experience is merely the natural and necessary assumption that what we learn of our surroundings will continue to serve as a reliable basis for future encounters. But repetitions of childhood happenings tend to occur in therapy in such rigid, persistent and dramatic form that Freud was led to seek further explanation for them.

He developed two concepts: 'regression' and 'repetition-compulsion'. Regression takes place at times when present-day life is too harsh and frightening to confront: the person takes refuge in a mode of functioning – that of the child – which is simpler, well-tried and calculated to evoke helpful responses in those around. The repetition-compulsion is a primary, elemental urge to repeat all past experience, and reaches its culmination in the wish to die, thereby returning to the state of inanimate matter. These formulations, particularly the former, have, together with the recognition that traumatic situations may be repeated in order to gain mastery of them, carried sufficient explanatory weight to serve psychotherapy well. But something vital is omitted if the child (and patient) is conceived merely as an entity which, in a rather mechanical way, takes the least line of resistance and retreats to a safe position. There is no sense of a risky and hopeful return to a position before discouragement and defeat had gained the upper hand, or indication of a trustful yearning to find, in another, the truth and possibility which had been never found. It is as though an observer, watching a child shrinking back from a strange dog, saying, 'Please, Mummy, I want to stroke him, but hold my hand' were to be more impressed by his fear than his courage.

In recent years, owing to the work of Winnicott,[1] Balint,[2] Milner,[3] Rycroft,[4] Khan[5] and others, there has been increasing recognition of the *realistic hope* contained in regressive tendencies. Their work implies that the child is less in a state of retreat than of confusion, less an experimental rat avoiding a painful stimulation than a person distraught by an apparently meaningless situation yet endeavouring to make sense of it. Winnicott, as I have already mentioned, conceives of a 'true self', which, although in retreat, is awaiting its opportunity to make a further exploration into the world, should more favourable conditions present themselves – a formulation which contrasts with the very great emphasis which most current psychoanalytic theory places on the defence against truth which is thought to characterize the 'abnormal' behaviour of mentally sick people (cf. Chapter 7).

I am emphasizing this point not only because it is clearly of vital importance in therapy to respond to hope but because, I believe, the failure to recognize the degree to which the patient searches for truth, meaning and relationship even in regressed behaviour exaggerates the difference between him and the therapist : it is a denigration of the patient comparable to that which adults make of children and which widens the gulf between the generations : it encourages the view that the therapist – as a seeker of the truth – is morally superior and it stands in the way of the acceptance by patient and therapist that they are ordinary and similar human beings.

What are the hurtful experiences which patients bring from their past? The idea that they are intolerable frustrations of sexuality and aggression, however important, is inadequate; and perhaps the experiences are too diverse to admit to easy generalization. But I would suggest the following classifications may be useful provided they are recognized as being intimately related :

(1) Experiences which diminish the child's belief in his own capacity and worth;
(2) Experiences which diminish the child's belief in the capacity of others to respond to and care for him.

While the first kind of experience leads the child into an unhealthy and excessive parasitic dependence, the latter forces him into a false independence – a self-sufficiency based on a resigned and cynical pessimism about what he might expect from others. Any attempt at therapy must confront these two inadequacies and provide a response which enables the patient to trust both himself and others. In effect it means that the therapist will only help if he perceives and respects the patient and can be trusted to give care when the latter reveals his true incapacity to function. Because the original failure was a human one (leaving aside such acts of God as death or enforced separation) so will the failures of the therapist be human ones rather than 'special' errors of technique. To the extent that he is rejecting, rigid, confused, indifferent, over-anxious, and so on, he will not be able to give the patient what is needed : the sense of his own value and the sense that there are others whom he can trust with both his adult and his childhood self. I shall return to the question of therapy in Chapter 8. For the remainder of this chapter I shall be concerned with the nature of the 'true self' to which the therapist must respond, and the ways in which it is concealed.

The 'true self' is a concept which has been used by several writers. I was myself first introduced to this formulation by the writings of Winnicott and it is his way of thinking about it that has most influenced me.

The true self, I take it, is that which develops directly from the original being of the child. It is imperfect and ill-defined (because we live in an imperfect and ill-defined world) but it remains roughly true to our innate potential. When, beyond a certain degree, the true self is so crushed or impoverished by the environment, it develops, for its own sake and for the sake of others, an alternative or false self which appears to function adequately.

The despair when no one responds to the true self can be seen in a poem by a fourteen-year-old boy, written shortly before he committed suicide, and read by Anne Allen at the Federation of Children's Book Groups :

He always
He always wanted to explain things, but no one
   cared.
So he drew.

Sometimes he would just draw and it wasn't
   anything.
He wanted to carve it in stone or write it in
   the sky.
He would lie out on the grass and look up in
   the sky and it would be only the sky and
   the things inside him that needed saying.

And it was after that that he drew the picture.
It was a beautiful picture. He kept it under
   his pillow and would let no one see it.
And he would look at it every night and think
   about it.
And when it was dark and his eyes were closed he
   could see it still.
And it was all of him and he loved it.

When he started school he brought it with him,
Not to show anyone, but just to have it with
   him like a friend.

It was funny about school.
He sat at a square brown desk like all the other
   square desks and he thought it would be red.
And his room was a square brown room, like all
   the other rooms.
And it was tight and close. And stiff.

He hated to hold the pencil and chalk, with
   his arm still and his feet flat on the floor,
   still, with the teacher watching and watching.

The teacher came and spoke to him.
She told him to wear a tie like all the other boys
He said he didn't like them and she said it
   didn't matter.

After that they drew. And he drew all yellow and
   it was the way he felt about morning. And
   it was beautiful.

The teacher came and smiled at him. 'What's this?'
she said.
'Why don't you draw something like Ken's drawing?
Isn't it beautiful?'
After that his mother bought him a tie and he
always drew airplanes and rocket-ships
like everyone else.

And he threw the old picture away.

And when he lay out alone looking at the sky,
it was big and blue, and all of everything,
but he wasn't anymore.

He was square and brown inside and his hands
were stiff.
And he was like everyone else. All the things
inside him that needed saying didn't need
it anymore.

It had stopped pushing. It was crushed.
Stiff.
Like everything else.

This child destroyed a life which was not worth living because it was utterly false; what was true had already died. But those who have not reached such a state of despair may hope that something may be preserved if they eliminate all that is false in them.

Again, the important contribution of Winnicott was to show how one of the functions of the false self was to act as a 'caretaker' to the true self, concealing and protecting it in the hope that one day circumstances may become sufficiently favourable for it (I should say 'me' or 'him' or 'her') to take a step into the world again.

In searching out the meaning of apparently pathological behaviour the therapist has to understand (and this, I think, can only be done at an intuitive level) the degree to which it signifies a hopeful exploration on behalf of the true self. The behaviour may, or may not, represent a retreat from creative living.

The retreat from true experience takes, I think, two forms. In so far as an activity is purely defensive – in the sense used by Freud – it is engaged upon simply to avoid (in fact or in imagination) the feared situation. It involves those techniques (denial, projection, displacement, etc.) which have been so well described in the psychoanalytical literature. On the other hand, a person may seek out alternative forms of experience less in an attempt to deny reality than to find meaning in something which is, of necessity, his second choice. The two manoeuvres may subtly interchange.

If John wants to be a pilot but for some reason is prevented from fulfilling this ambition, he may quickly decide that he would 'really' prefer to become an engineer in order, defensively, to deny the validity of his first choice. In addition, however, he will try to make the most of engineering for its own sake – to extract from the experience the most meaning he can, using the same interests and gifts that would have been applied to his original choice. (Freud used the term 'sublimation' to describe a successful transfer of this kind, particularly emphasizing the part played by similarity of form – what Susanne Langer[6] calls 'non-discursive symbolism' – between the two interests, and the significance of basic sexual urges.) If the transfer is not too successful, however, the person may be forced into using a considerable amount of energy and ingenuity in order to persuade himself (and others) that his second choice is 'really' meaningful. In some cases this attempt to create the impression of a meaningful life out of the ruins of a traumatic break with reality – holding, as it were, a carrot in front of one's nose in order to drive oneself on – may dominate the clinical picture. The efforts which a fetishistic patient may put into his attempts to create an interesting and exciting experience can, I think, only be described in this way.

The identification of motive can be important in practice. There is a significant difference between obsessional neatness designed to deny the existence of an urge to be dirty, and the creation of an obsessional way of life in order to exist in a meaningful world – 'having', as T. S. Eliot puts it, 'to construct something/Upon which to rejoice'.

Disturbed behaviour arising out of the hopeful urges of the crippled true self can also take different forms. Firstly, there is the 'caretaker' activity, which tries to ensure that the true self remains viable. Secondly, there is the search for more hopeful conditions, a search which, because of previous reverses, may take such tentative and distorted forms that its true meaning can easily be overlooked. For instance a patient may subject the therapist to all manner of tests with the aim of finding out if he can be trusted, yet such tests may be so severe that at first sight they appear to be motivated by a purely sadistic desire to discourage or destroy. Thirdly, there is an attack on the successful, although false, adaptation which has enabled the true self to survive hitherto but which must now be sloughed off in order that a return to true experience can become possible. This last type of hopeful behaviour is particularly confusing and I shall elaborate on it.

A successful analysis, or similar therapeutic endeavour, includes, as one of its consequences, the elimination of those parts of the personality which stand in the way of healthy development: that which is false and sterile has to go. In many cases the dead and diseased wood is gradually shed during the course of treatment. In some more severe character disorders the defensive shell of the personality (the 'false self') is so securely embedded and necessary to life that it can only be removed by drastic measures. Indeed, neither patient nor therapist may consciously desire to alter a highly-organized and culturally-adapted personality structure: such a change would have to be forced upon both of them.

For a change of this kind to be made, two requirements must be met: firstly, a setting must be provided which enables the patient to survive the transient psychological disruption. He must be 'held' by the psychotherapist and others during the period of his weakness, when the true self has not yet had time to become established in the world.

Secondly, a means must be found of disturbing or destroying an adaptive but sterile way of living. The psychotherapist

D

may, by his interpretations, enable a person to see the kind of change that is necessary, but in some cases may not be able to initiate it. There are several ways by means of which this necessary change – the destruction of the false self – can be induced. These include certain religious practices, drugs, illnesses or accidents. The following is an example of a person who used illness for this purpose.

A few months after the termination of an analysis that had seemed to be fairly satisfactory, Roy became ill. The illness started slowly in that he felt anxious, frail and slightly unreal for a few weeks before it manifested itself. Then, one day, he felt so ill that he went to his general practitioner, who found that he had a very slight temperature and a rapid pulse. By the next day he was in a state of collapse and was taken to hospital, hardly able to raise his head from the pillow, convinced that he was dying. His medical advisers (with whom I was later in touch) were rather concerned about him, but apart from a very rapid pulse and a transient abnormality in the electro-cardiograph no satisfactory explanation could be found for his extremely frail condition; after a week in hospital he was returned home. Although he gradually improved, almost any action caused palpitations, tremors, and unpleasant sensations in the testicles. Mental effort was also difficult, he had frequent nightmares and began to realize that he was suffering from some kind of psychological breakdown. As soon as he was physically able he came to see me and analysis was resumed. Some interesting facts about his illness then emerged.

A few weeks before his illness started Roy had had a dream about a man who had an operation for a brain tumour but, although the head had been neatly sewn up again, the tumour remained inside. At about this time, without any conscious knowledge that he was about to become ill, he started to make elaborate provision for the event, arranging his finances and organizing his work as though he were going away for a long holiday.

During the course of his illness, which lasted about two months, Roy was less guarded, and interpretative work was easier, than when he had come for analysis previously. However, his steady improvement – that is to say, his readaptation to the environment – appeared to be unrelated to the insights he gained during any particular session and had an inexorably gradual quality. I shall leave aside the analysis of the many life-long conflicts which emerged in more vivid form than before, and focus on the actual 'illness' and the meaning we came to attribute to it. The main features of his state of mind at this time were as follows.

Roy was very confused and emotional, feared that he was going insane, was at times depersonalized, and was unable to attach meaning to those aspects of his life which normally attracted his interest – a loss of mental control which was accompanied by comparable physical changes : disturbances of pulse rate, temperature regulation and sleep rhythm. During the crisis he became intensely preoccupied with his state of health, imagined himself to be suffering from various fatal illnesses and kept constant check on the functions of his body and mind. Although these phenomena could be interpreted, following Freud, as an increased narcissism following a withdrawal of interest in the outside world, it would seem that his self-preoccupation was, to some extent, realistic : he was concerned with the manner of his functioning (and particularly with the need to conserve energy) because he could no longer function adequately.

At times – either out of impatience or shame or in response to interpretations of his passivity (which was quite a formidable feature of his psychopathology) – Roy tried to increase the pace of his return to normality, but each effort in this direction produced a recurrence of severe symptoms. At first I thought this was a masochistic manoeuvre – a punishment for his desire to attain health and all that this meant in terms of competitive success – but I came to the conclusion that he was permitting his true self to grow at its own pace and was destroying, by means of his symptoms, any attempt on the part of the false self to regain its position.

For the first few weeks of his illness Roy was abjectly

dependent on those around him – especially myself, his doctor and his wife. Like several features of his psychological state, the dependence on others seemed to be a consequence of his confusion and disintegration; he had lost his way, could no longer rely on his own maps and desperately sought a guide. In this state he was less narcissistic than hitherto, and prepared, with more humility and attention than before, to listen to the views of those around him (although at times he became fearful that others would take advantage of or mismanage his weak and dependent state, and he became paranoid and hostile).

In his normal state Roy was a conscientious man, a hard worker keen to have the approval of others and to be regarded as a good, reliable, steady citizen and husband. Now these aims were lost. He ceased to care deeply about worldly success or to harass himself with the needs and expectations of others; in a sense he became more selfish. Although at first all effort was impossible, it gradually became clear that there was a certain amount of selection taking place; he was quite unable to do anything to please, or perform any action that could be considered to be in the category of work. I felt that the main feature of this process was the collapse of a drive that lacked spontaneity, that was compulsive and socially conditioned. He became selfish in that he determined (or was forced by his illness) to do only that which he felt genuinely and truly to emerge from his own being.

At times Roy became so overwhelmed by destructive urges that he continued to exist and maintain his relationships only in the hope that these urges might lessen. Before the breakdown, he had contrived in various ways to make his life purposeful. In the crisis in which he now found himself the manoeuvres he had hitherto used to create an impression of meaning were no longer possible to him; as a consequence he was lost, apathetic, depressed, enraged and humiliated, but behind these extraordinarily frightening and painful feelings he persisted in a hope that he was at last 'finding himself'.

The main difficulty in understanding this kind of process,

which involves so much ambiguity, is to distinguish the positive and negative elements : is one witnessing the emergence of a true self or a compulsive, bitter, uncreative withdrawal from and revolt against an adaptation to life which is no longer tenable?

One guide to the positive element in the process was my patient's dreams, of which the following is an example :

A man was running in a race. There were thousands of spectators. Round and round the track they went, seemingly without end. He kept in the lead, but only just. Suddenly he fell to the ground. I was astounded and horrified. Surely this couldn't be; he *must* win. I ran over to him. But to my surprise he hadn't actually collapsed involuntarily : he had decided he wasn't going to continue driving himself on just for the benefit of the spectators – an absurd and crippling thing to do. Immediately, I changed my own view and felt that he was right. I congratulated him on his courage.

Then the dream changed and I was holding a baby in my arms. We seemed to be in harmony with each other and everything we did was in accord with the rhythm of a tune I was singing. I had a sense of vigour and strength in the baby.

In describing the process I have oversimplified. It was much more confused, confusing and ambiguous than I have conveyed. Nor did it resolve itself smartly and successfully; there was no metamorphosis from false to true. Indeed, this 'illness' was only the first – albeit the most dramatic – of several which occurred over the course of three to four years. The general pattern of change was a positive one and in terms of personal integration and of sincerity of purpose this was, in the main, a creative effort. But it also represented in several ways a degree of destruction, failure and limitation. The process was performed at quite a cost to those around him, and involved risk : it might not have paid off. Even if there had been no distortion of the nature of the process – that is, even if it had been recognized as a psychological crisis and not an illness – it would still have been costly, but the presentation of an 'illness' made matters worse. Moreover, in place of a relatively smooth psychological transition Roy had periods of enormous confusion and mistrust during which he made savage attacks on those around him, using his incapacity as a weapon.

Roy's abandonment of the techniques of the false self was as much forced upon him as it was a creative decision. He had reached an age in life (mid-life) at which not only was he sufficiently established socially to allow such a crisis to occur, but also he no longer possessed the physical and psychological energy to maintain the sterile defensive system which had served him in the past.

The attack on the false self which I have just described took the form of a physical and mental collapse which undermined the whole tenor of a previous way of life and occurred in the context of psychotherapy. But attacks of this kind may take quite different and often more abortive forms and be much less well organized. I would like now to consider the ways in which such an attack may be the reason for some of the symptoms of anorexia nervosa (a condition in which the patient suffers complete loss of appetite and, if female [which is typical of the disease] ceases to menstruate).

In two cases of anorexia nervosa I was struck by the various ways in which the patient attacked her own body. Refusal to eat and loss of sexual function may both be conceived as ways of destroying the body as a whole or certain characteristics which it possesses. In both patients there were additional features which confirmed this view. Both were addicted to purgatives, and in each case this seemed to derive from a violent and self-destructive urge to scour out the inside of the body – to destroy everything that was bad and to become cleansed and pure. Everything that was incorporated into the body was felt to be alien, dangerous and impure : hence the tendency towards refusal of food and the need to get rid of the latter as soon as possible. In Melanie Klein's conceptual scheme : a 'bad object' (bad because of the aggression projected upon it) had been taken in and was existing within as something poisonous and persecuting. This way of putting it, however, leaves out of account the shame and self-disgust at having been seduced into accepting and incorporating a world felt to be alien, and the determination to destroy the capacity to continue in this false position. In one of these patients the emphasis was on eating, which symbolized a false acceptance of the world in order to survive and please; the other patient had been seduced into using her body as a vehicle to gain love. But the two different emphases were closely intermingled; eating comes into the area of sexuality once it is linked, in a woman's mind, with the attempt to mould her figure into a desirable shape. If one recognizes the oversimplification, anorexia nervosa can be thought of as a malignant form of dieting. At one stroke the mother who tells her daughter to eat and grow big and (later) to make herself pretty and please men is confounded and the false self which has agreed to these proposals is annulled.

I would now like to give an example of a patient who came to me almost out of the blue, who used a drug to precipitate the kind of change I am describing and who, because of her freshness to psychotherapeutic thought, described her conflict in a particularly unadulterated way.

Miss B., a young woman in her early twenties, came to me for a consultation to discuss whether she should have a course of psychotherapy. We agreed, after the interview, that she should. I had no vacancy myself and the therapist who I thought would be suitable had just gone on a month's holiday. I told her I would approach him on his return. She left, with rather a sad smile, and I felt a little uneasy about her. Perhaps I had picked up – or, rather, failed to pick up – that she could not wait a month.

Two weeks later Miss B. rang me in a state of such anxiety that she could hardly speak. 'I *know* now,' she said, 'I *know* now. I'm *nothing*. I took mescalin last night. I don't know how to go on.' I suggested she come to see me and she agreed eagerly.

Her appearance and manner this time were very different. She was dishevelled and distraught, gripped her chair with her hands as if to find something with which to hold herself together, and spoke in short sentences, emphasizing many words. It is difficult for me to convey the complete absence of hysteria from this emotional outburst. She spoke simply, humbly and with convincing sincerity. 'Now I *know* what I *am.* Everything I have *ever* done has been to *please* people. But I didn't ask to be born, did I? A plastic bag was put on me and I couldn't get out of it. Is that the womb or what is it? I've *never* escaped from my mother. I'm just her and there's nothing of me. I can only go on living if I forget all about this. Otherwise it's just a vacuum, emptiness, *nothing.* I've got to forget this if I can fit in again. My life's all been tricks. I never stop trying to make people like me.'

'But you aren't trying at this moment,' I said.

'No, I'm not trying now, but I'm nothing.'

'No, you're not nothing. The nothing bit brought you here. You wanted to share it.'

She looked relieved. 'Yes, that's true.'

Later in the session she started to talk about her body.

'I *hate* my body. I *hate* it. It's all lies. I've always asked my body to pretend. Tom says I've a beautiful body – but it's all false. I want to take it off or get rid of it or kill it or something. I can't be *me* with this body. They put the wrong body on the wrong person and it doesn't fit.

'And there's another mix-up. I've got to be *pure.* I've got to have a *pure* body – yet I've got to please people sexually as well. It's two opposites. *There's* a hang-up for you. I've got to please people one way or another. And *I* do all this to *myself.* That's the *worst* thing.'

I said: 'But you only do it because you've been forced into it.'

'Yes – I can't see any other way to live. . . . I've never escaped from my mother. I *am* her. Everything I do is to please her – although she doesn't know it. . . .

'I want to tell everyone about this, but I won't. This afternoon I told someone and he just buttoned it up. "You've always played tricks" he said: "Now you can stop. You'll be a lot better." I wanted to scream.'

I saw her once again a few days later. Although feeling empty and exhausted she had calmed down and spoke of the vital importance to her of not forgetting the insights gained during her psychological crisis.

The circumstances which precipitate an attack on the false self are of two rather different kinds. In a time of hope – when he either has established a sufficiently secure position in the world to be able to give it up for a while, or sees the opportunity of being understood and cared for if he drops his defences – a person may organize an attack on the false self to allow the true self to appear. In other cases, a person may become unable to use his defensive system in order to make a socially adequate adaptation. During the course of the breakdown he may, in bitterness and disillusionment, attack the ways of adapting which have, in the end, proved false – but perhaps with the desperate hope that, if they can be completely eradicated, something new will emerge. From the point of view of psychotherapy, it is, of course, the recognition of hope that is necessary. For this reason it is important to distinguish a creative attack upon the false elements in the self from other forms of self-destruction. These forms include the following :

(1) Global, primitive aggression, which includes the self in its blind attack;
(2) Blocked aggression redirected towards the self, as when a person tears his hair for want of another target;
(3) Identification with the aggressor (cf. Anna Freud[7]) : vicarious satisfaction in the sadism of the attacker;
(4) Self-destruction to comply with the unconscious wishes of the parents;
(5) Immediate destruction of anything good or creative in order to forestall disappointment;
(6) Self-punishment to alleviate guilt;
(7) Self-destruction to make others have mercy, feel guilty or take pity; and the internalization of this pattern, which then constitutes 'moral masochism', as conceived by Freud;

D*

(8) Destructive disintegration of the self to avoid the pain of complete experience : cf. Melanie Klein;[8]

(9) The severing of those parts of the self which link the person with the outer world : cf. Bion;[9]

(10) Self-destruction for the purpose of depriving others of the satisfaction of having oneself to love;

(11) The repetition of a traumatic attack on oneself in order to master the anxiety and pain which could not be accepted in the past;

(12) Addiction of self-destructive activities which have (purposefully) become associated with physical pleasure; in Freud's term, 'erotogenic masochism'.

Finally, I would like to draw attention to the sense of loss and guilt that may be experienced in different ways by people who have abandoned their true selves and see no hope of recovery : the mourning over the childhood self which has failed to develop. Patients often have dreams in which they are trying desperately to save a child who is lost, drowning, suffocating, et cetera. Such dreams are usually felt with great poignancy. A patient who over the course of several years' analysis kept a stiff upper lip in the English tradition, broke down and cried about half a dozen times; on each occasion this was precipitated by a dream of such a nature, the associations of which could usually be traced to himself as a small child. It may be that parents' anxieties about the survival of their children – notably those of mothers in the post-natal period – may have this origin and sometimes be mistakenly attributed to aggressive wishes towards the child.

Edwin Muir's beautiful poem, 'The Child Dying', is, I feel, a mourning for this kind of loss.

> *Unfriendly friendly universe,*
> *I pack your stars into my purse,*
> *And bid you, bid you so farewell.*
> *That I can leave you, quite go out,*
> *Go out, go out beyond all doubt,*
> *My father says, is the miracle.*

You are so great, and I so small:
I am nothing, you are all:
Being nothing, I can take this way.
Oh I need neither rise nor fall,
For when I do not move at all
I shall be out of all your day.

It's said some memory will remain
In the other place, grass in the rain,
Light on the land, sun on the sea,
A flitting grace, a phantom face,
But the world is out. There is no place
Where it and its ghost can ever be.

Father, father, I dread this air
Blown from the far side of despair,
The cold cold corner. What house, what hold,
What hand is there? I look and see
Nothing-filled eternity,
And the great round world grows weak and old.

Hold my hand, oh hold it fast –
I am changing! – until at last
My hand in yours no more will change,
Though yours change on. You here, I there,
So hand in hand, twin-leafed despair –
I did not know death was so strange.

Guilt may be felt towards the true self not only because it has been buried and forgotten in a morass of defences but on occasions when it is exposed to situations in which it is too frail to survive (cf. Woodmansey[10]). This is most evident when, in the course of therapy, the true self has again begun to grow but in so doing has become vulnerable to trauma. This phenomena suggests that children may intuitively recognize the danger to their growth of a traumatic situation and this knowledge enters into the ferocity and anguish of their feelings. Perhaps this is what Martin, whose case I shall describe in the next chapter, meant when, out of the blue, he said to his mother 'You blocked me, Mummy'.

7

The Attempt to Resolve Confusion

Without consideration, without pity, without shame
They have built big and high walls around me.
And now I sit here despairing
I think of nothing else: this fate gnaws at my mind;
For I had many things to do outside.
Ah why didn't I observe them when they were building the
*   walls?*
But I never heard the noise or the sound of the builders.
Imperceptibly they shut me out of the world.
C. P. CAVAFY translated by RAE DALVEN

There are two main theories about the psychological origins of mental illness: the 'defence theory' and the 'confusion theory'.

The 'defence theory', which was originated by Freud, asserts that a person becomes ill because he denies reality: his wishes – and the fears which are the consequence of his wishes – are so powerful that they interfere with his capacity to perceive true reality: he cannot integrate these two facets of experience – wish and reality – and the split between them is incapacitating. The therapeutic task is to overcome the person's defences against accepting reality – weaning him from his outrageous desire, and leading him through the straight and narrow path to satisfactory adaptation.

The 'confusion theory', which springs from various sources,

but has had its major impetus in the work on schizophrenic families in the past two decades, asserts that a person becomes ill when others present reality to him in such a confusing way that it is impossible for him to make sense of it.

These two theories are, to my mind, unquestionably correct and must be compatible. What has so far prevented them from becoming assimilated to each other is not only the fact that, in the field of psychotherapy, differing ideas do not readily and happily intermix, but that each theory tends to take sides (without this necessarily being apparent) in the eternal dialogue between youth and age. Whereas defence theory, which stresses the child's unwillingness to adapt, is on the side of the adult, confusion theory, by focusing on the failure of the family, is on the side of the child. And just as parents and children do not easily agree, so it is with the supporters of their various viewpoints and rights. When the lion and the lamb lie down together, we may expect Colonel Blimp and Jean-Jacques Rousseau to be bed-mates. In this chapter I shall discuss the ways in which these two theories, as they are presented at the present time, fail to provide an adequate basis for psychotherapy. It is appropriate to start with the defence theory as this continues to dominate clinical practice.

The inequality with which we structure our world is nowhere more unthinkingly accepted than in the relationship between adult and child. This century has seen a major assault upon the presumptions of adults, but, with the advent of 'the permissive society', a reaction appears to be setting in, and much of the present unrest is blamed upon leniency towards the young; child-centred upbringing is now some-times regarded, even in liberal circles, as a little outdated – a worthy ideal which has been allowed to get a bit out of hand. This reaction is, as I suggested earlier, a characteristic phase in changing philosophies: the inevitable disruption which is a symptom of change, the distortions by extremists among the reformers, and the consequence of reforms which go far enough to awaken dissatisfied urges, yet not far enough to assuage them, all these combine to make an unhappy state of affairs and bring disrepute upon the philosophy of the movement.

It may seem surprising, in view of Freud's contribution to the ethos of permissive child-rearing, to criticize his theory for its failure to narrow the gulf between parent and child; but the paradox of Freud is that his genius led him to recognize the child's emotional needs yet he never quite emancipated himself from an authoritarian attitude towards these needs. He revealed our hypocrisy – our attempt to believe that we are better than nature made us. His arguments are telling; there is much evidence supporting the theory that we have an innate tendency to distort; but we must not allow ourselves to be entirely crushed by the evidence which this theory has at its disposal. Freud's assertion that the child is possessed by omnipotent desires which he can be persuaded to abandon only after a cataclysmic struggle, and, correspondingly, that the adult in psychotherapy must be freed from unrealistic aims by the interpretation of his defences against awareness of these aims, continues to dominate therapeutic practice and must be challenged. It is a theory which gives undue prominence to one kind of perceptual distortion to the neglect of others of equal or possibly even greater significance.

When perceiving the world about him, a person aims, as Gestalt psychology has shown, to arrange in as harmonious and meaningful a way as possible whatever impinges upon him. This endeavour will include organizing his field of perception in order to make it appear more in accord with urgent needs than it really is : a hungry man will see food where it is not. But the field will also be distorted to avoid confusions of *all* kinds : gross incompatibilities will, if possible, be given some kind of order. It is perhaps in the area of *intellectual* understanding that this phenomenon has most thoroughly been studied. Festinger[1] has shown the formidable persistence and ingenuity with which people will try to minimize disturbing incongruities of thought and opinion. When, for instance, one makes a definite decision after a period of conflict about a matter, the previous arguments against the decision taken usually appear less telling. Much that Festinger describes is similar to the technique known to psychoanalysts as 'rationalization' (the spurious justification of views and actions whose true nature one needs to conceal) but in the latter case it is assumed, in keeping with basic Freudian theory (which I am here questioning) that the significant discrepancy is between wish and reality, whereas Festinger is concerned with any and every incompatibility in the field. It would seem that the Freudian theory of conflict should be extended : if the elements in the perceptual field are disparate beyond a certain degree then the person will not be able to organize them and may become seriously confused, which results in what is usually described as 'psychopathology' or 'mental illness'.

According to Freud there is a continuous development in the manner of resolving conflict : the infant starts by giving preference to his own requirements and only gradually and painfully recognizes as real those aspects of the world which frustrate his physical urges. The child is seen, in Freud's view, in a quite extraordinarily negative way, as an entity which responds to life by recoiling away from any difficulty, which neither knows nor pursues the truth, and which is reluctantly persuaded to see the truth by the force of circumstances, primarily the admonitions of the adult world. Growth is forced upon him.

It cannot of course be denied that the child learns much from adults and in so doing gives up views which he previously held. But in the process of learning he, to some extent, gives up his previous aims not because they *were* inappropriate but because they *have become* inappropriate in the new state of his increased growth : his old aims have not been discredited in favour of 'reality'. Secondly, when a child gives up aims in favour of the dictates of his family or of society it is by no means certain which of the two viewpoints is reasonable – whether in fact he or his family had the greater hold on reality – for within the *range* of his appropriate experience he has as appreciable a chance of being correct as those around him, because, although his perceptual apparatus is not well-developed, it operates from a unique and strategic position. He is, for example, in a better position than his mother or the paediatrician to know whether he is experiencing pain. In many ways he may be in the best position to know what would be the most appropriate response to his own being, but he has to leave it to others to deal with Herod, Hitler or the meningococcus.

There are several reasons, then, why Freud failed to take sufficiently into account, in formulating a theory of psycho-pathology, the sources of confusion in the child's environment. Firstly, he put too great an emphasis on the avoidance of pain, as opposed to loss of meaning, as the important traumatic factor; secondly, he believed that confusion is inherent to the child because of his conflicting aims between wish and 'reality', and thirdly, his adult-centred view did not allow him to realize that the child has to decide at every stage of development whether his own perceptions of those around him are correct – that is, it is not a question of the child's simply learning reality with the help of parents whose own correctness of perception can be taken for granted.

Although 'object-relations theory' (cf. Chapter 5, pp. 66–8) corrects the view that the child's primary aim is the relief of instinctual tension and establishes the fact that he seeks a personal relationship, it retains Freud's theory that the other person is seen by the child primarily as a source of satisfaction and that he becomes confused when faced with the problem of feeling both love and hate towards the *same* person (primarily his mother), a conflict that he avoids by splitting the image of his mother into two people : a 'good' mother and a 'bad' mother. Even Fairbairn, who has done more than any other analyst to establish the idea that the child is a primarily integrated meaningful whole, subscribes to the view that he is inherently disposed to become confused – that his only response to frustration is to split.[2]

The failure to recognize the predicament of a child faced with a need to harmonize the confusions around him has led psychoanalysts to exaggerate the importance of the 'inter-

nalization' of the parents during the course of ordinary development. That such internalization occurs is not in doubt : the
child relies, to greater or lesser degree, on mental representa-
tions of significant people providing a source of strength and
security to him. But, as it stands, the theory, in stating that the
child's personality structure is *primarily* built upon the internalization of the parent, gives undue prominence to the latter's
influence in a *healthy* set-up. Moreover, it attributes the dis-
harmony which an internalized figure can cause a child to
the vicissitudes of his uncontrollable passions (for example, the
projection of his hate on to the internalized figure, which
thereupon becomes threatening) rather than to confusion of
viewpoint between the child and his actual, real-life parent.

This last factor is one which should not be underestimated.
One of the difficulties facing a child is that he is inevitably
confronted with the presence, within his own field of perception, of another and a very potent perceiving figure : his parent.
He is forced to use this other mind, for certain purposes, as
though it were his own : to be dependent on it and, to a degree,
identify with it, and yet to be able to distinguish it from his
own.

It would seem to be more likely that the child's personality
grows because of the gradual assimilation of experience, including the experience of his relationship with his parents and of
their viewpoint, into the basic Gestalt (the meaningful whole)
of his personality. Only when the parents' influence is over-
whelming will it be sufficiently imprinted on him for one to
say that his personality has been formed on the basis of internalization. It is inevitable that the viewpoint of the parents
will often be accepted by the child before he is sufficiently
experienced to assess it, and it is inevitable that sometimes
this viewpoint will be mistaken and will clash with other
experience and cause a degree of confusion, but in a realistic
set-up such confusion will be peripheral rather than central
and will not lead to the presence, in his mind, of internalized
figures which overpower his capacity to think and act for
himself. When, however, the discrepancy between the view-

point of the child and of the parents is too great for him to
assimilate them into a meaningful whole, he is forced to
abandon this aim and to form separate, incompatible Gestalts,
one or more of which continuously threaten to invalidate his
own perception. This, I believe, is the main reason why the
'internalized object' is so often felt by the child as a threat –
whether or not it becomes a source of projected aggression.
Moreover, in regarding the nature of the 'internalized object'
as largely a function of the child's impulses, psychoanalytic
theory fails to encompass the fact that in practice most psychoanalysts pay great attention to the viewpoint and action of the
parents and recognize that what a child internalizes depends
on the actuality of the particular parent concerned : psychoanalysts are, I believe, usually interested in and sensitive to the
general mood and atmosphere in which a child grows up.
Family atmosphere is not easy to define or incorporate
into theory, yet, if the predicament of the child is to be understood, must be confronted. The child's capacity for testing
reality is put at risk not only by the confusing manner in
which *specific* communications are made to him – for instance,
the discrepancy between verbal and non-verbal messages – but
also by a false presentation of 'reality' on the part of his
parents. A consistent and well-organized presentation of 'reality'
which is in fact wrong will be confusing to the child – indeed,
the better the presentation the more convincing, and therefore
more disturbing, it will be. Such a presentation can, of course,
occur even before the child learns to speak : the way he is
handled, the manner in which the parents go about their affairs,
the whole emotional tone of family life involve implicit asser-
tions about the child, the parents, and the nature of existence.
A depressed mother cannot but help invalidating the naturally
lively and optimistic yearnings and beliefs of her child,
although the child's unsullied perception of the world will in
many respects be a more realistic one than that of his unhappy
parent. This area of study – the conflict between parents and
child – has in many ways already been charted by psychoanalysis, but much of it will have to be rewritten in a different

language and with a different emphasis if the reality – as well as the fantasy – of the relationship is to be taken into consideration.

The traditional theory of psychotherapeutic practice leans heavily not only on the belief that the patient (like the child) is primarily concerned to defend himself against truth, but that in a successful treatment the patient 'internalizes' the therapist in the way that a child is believed to internalize his parents. The consequences of this theory go deep.

There is a danger that, by accepting Freud's view in this matter, the psychotherapist may be too inclined to regard his patient's words and actions as defences against reality and, in particular, as resistances to accepting the 'reality' of his interpretations. If this occurs, then an adult-centred view of the child engenders a therapist-centred view of the patient; the latter's genuine striving towards meaning and truth are underestimated. This is a theme to which I shall return in the next chapter, but I would like to give a short illustration of what I mean.

At our first session a patient told me that he would not be able to pay my usual fee (to which he had previously agreed). After some discussion we settled on a slightly reduced fee. Some weeks later he asked if he could have slightly longer sessions. I pointed out his tendency to try to obtain a little more than the original agreement in these two ways, and it became possible for me to understand the meaning of this, and for him to accept my interpretation. He thereupon ceased asking for extra time and agreed to my usual fee.

Shortly after this interchange he had a dream about a complacent tyrannical psychiatrist who (like his father) was 'always right', and who would have him put away if he disagreed with him. It was clear, from certain details in the dream, that the psychiatrist represented myself. During our discussion of the dream the patient said ruefully 'You are always right, aren't you? You were right about the money.' I suggested to him that although my specific interpretation had been useful, this had no real bearing on the 'correctness' of the fee and length of sessions, which were quite arbitrary matters: who was to say what I should charge him? I also pointed out that he had assumed that my only motive in making the interpretations was the pure one of concern for his mental well-being, that he had been unable to recognize my own self-interested desire to take some more of his money from him. I must have said this in a way that convinced him of the reality of my mercenary tendencies, for he became immensely relieved and relaxed, and laughed for several minutes.

This sort of confrontation is a daily occurrence in most family situations. When the parent says 'You must do it this way, because . . .' the healthy child intuitively knows that he is dealing with a being like himself whose motives must be questioned. The child who is too frightened or confused to formulate such questions may find himself in the psycho-therapist's consulting-room twenty years later. But it would be ironic, and tragic, if factors in the new situation lessened his chances of emancipation from the assumption that the other is always right.

If one focuses less on the patient's defences against reality, other of his aims or possible aims come into view. Many forms of distorted, pathological functioning usually regarded as defences against reality may, in fact, be direct consequences of the confusing environment to which he has been subjected in early life. The child who has been confused by others becomes incapable of a direct approach to the truth; but his difficulties in assessing reality depend on his distorted perceptions, his attempts to defend these and his endeavour by devious measures to find his way to the truth which evades him, rather than on a primary shrinking from the truth.

No less important are the limitations of potential which do not depend on defensive operations but have simply not been awakened by the environment. The assumptions, or lack of assumptions, with which he was met have prevented him from perceiving the possibilities open to him.

Our perceptions do not lie exclusively in the present, but

incorporate experience of the past and assumptions about the future. I see this page as a unit not only in space but in time, as though it existed, at least for a few seconds, both before and after my glance. In the case of entities which have intrinsic potential – such as people – our perception of them includes whatever we think them capable of doing as well as whatever they are actually doing. This assumption about capacities applies also to self-perception. I can walk only because I assume I can walk. If I could not make this assumption my picture of the world would disintegrate to such an extent that I would fall in a heap on the floor.

A child, whose self-perception is only in the process of growth, is particularly dependent on what people around him assume about him. What he can do depends on what others believe he can do. What is real to him is that which depends on his past and present experience and that which derives from assumptions, expectations, and faith possessed by himself and others.

To challenge the basic assumptions which others make about his capacities beyond a certain point is unthinkable and destroys his self-image : if, for instance, a mother takes it for granted that her daughter cannot live away from her (and no one else comes to the rescue) then the daughter will either herself believe and reveal that she cannot do so or will make the break by means of a pretence which may not sustain her for very long. Healthy exploration consists of a gradual expansion based on careful testing-out of one's capacities. Explorations beyond this range – fantasies – are not unduly disturbing provided they are not confused with potential reality. A child who is not provided with a basic perceptual framework in which to understand himself must, of necessity, use the greater part of his efforts – at the expense of normal growth – in trying to establish this framework; he will be preoccupied with testing reality.

A child's behaviour may be unduly restricted because of his fear of his parents, and this fear may be increased by his projection of his own aggression on to his parents; he may, in addition, harshly limit his aims out of fear of harming the parent by his aggression. But this formulation – the traditional Freudian and Kleinian one – leaves out of account the limitation placed upon the child by the failure of the parents to perceive him correctly and thereby give him a fruitful perceptual framework. (I shall give an illustration of this shortly – the case of Martin, p. 124.)

The difference between failing to recognize the potentialities of the child and attempting to limit them is probably crucial. In the first case the child will tend to accept his parents' belief that he has x capacity. Because there is no recognition of an x + n potential, his perceptual field will not contain n. If any flickering of n might appear, it will be annulled by the complete absence of response. This, I believe, may be an important element in the gross failure of potentiality that is known as mental subnormality. For this to happen, it does not necessarily mean that the parents have an unduly low estimate of this child; their expectations may, however, be so wide of the mark that the child virtually receives no validation of his potentialities and gets no sense of them as realities. If this is the case, the potentially gifted child may, through lack of recognition of his difference, fail to achieve normal development.

When it occurs to a lesser degree, this limitation of the perceptual field leads to a relative lack of imagination. A person afflicted in this way is spared many agonies of decision and his life expectations do not include the possibility of enrichment by psychotherapeutic exploration – so he is unlikely to consult a psychotherapist. In practice, however, patients often reveal a primary, deep-seated limitation of hope and imagination and do, in fact, get an appropriate response from their therapist; that is to say, the patient is encouraged to hope for more and to develop his perception of what might be (as in play therapy or art therapy), but the therapist does not recognize in his theories what he is doing, and believes that improvement in the patient's imaginative capacity is due to interpretation and not to encouragement.

Limitation of growth is not confined to the intellectual sphere. Feeling, like thought, is complex, and in order for it to exist with full intensity, it needs an environment to flourish in. In the case of certain feelings – concern, for instance – this necessity is recognized by psychoanalysis, but it is usually believed that other emotions, such as anger or anxiety or those associated with appetite, are 'instinctual' and primitive, and diminish rather than grow with time. But is it not more likely that even 'primitive' emotions require a setting in which they appear appropriate if they are to develop? If appetite receives no fulfilment, it will atrophy; but the more that life offers, the more the child feels encouragement to seek and the more his imagination plays on the possibilities around him. The more he realizes the possibilities of action, the more he feels anger when these are denied to him, in contrast to the child who, like the medieval serf, has not learned to appreciate his 'rights'. And the same with anxiety : when a large number of choices are open to a person, he is in the anxious position of having to make a complicated and effective choice, unlike someone who lacks freedom of choice (either for external reasons or because of a limitation of imaginative perception) and who may accept the inevitable automatically and without anxiety.

Limitation of growth occurs, I believe, whenever the parent 'keeps the child in his place' in the traditional Western manner of upbringing : that is to say, whenever the parent conceives of the child as essentially different from himself. I would like to give an example of this.

Miss R., an only child, was brought up by parents who were kind and responsible but did not fully share their lives with her. Decisions affecting the child were made without her participation and she was allotted a well-defined place in the household in which, it was assumed, she would be quite contented.

In her sessions with me this well-defined place was soon apparent. My area of the consulting-room was sacrosanct and it was as though there was an 'invisible glass wall between us'. She recalled that, in childhood, she had felt that children and adults were like two different kinds of animal; it had never really occurred to her that one could grow into the other. Later she compared her feeling as a child with having been a 'second-class citizen, with no vote and liable to expulsion from the club if he transgresses the unspoken rules, someone who is praised not for what he does but as though to say: "Fancy him being able to do that seeing he's only a black. . . ."

It was not surprising that Miss R. came to me because she lacked the initiative to use her potential. She had a good mind and could undertake most tasks competently and question much that went on around her. But she could never make the ultimate confrontation about her status and potential: others organized her life and she worked within the limits they set.

Any therapeutic endeavour with a person whose possibilities have been curtailed by the early assumptions of his parents is best thought of as a relationship which permits the growth of these possibilities. The interpretations of the patient's defences and the technical procedures which figure so much in the literature of psychotherapy will play far less a part than a personal relationship which permits and encourages spontaneity and growth. Some of the more recent psychoanalytic work shows acute awareness of those areas of the psychotherapeutic experience which call into account the *defence* theory of personality, but (as I mentioned in Chapter 5) it does not entirely emancipate itself from the theory as a whole. Other theories have arisen, outside the traditional movement, which, by contrast, place emphasis directly on the *confusion* to which the child – and, later, the patient – is subjected. I shall now consider these.

The American studies on the family – the work of Lidz,[3] Bateson,[4] Lynn[5] and others – which have been so stimulating in this area of thought, have focused mainly on schizophrenia, and what has emerged from this work is less a comprehensive theory of personality and treatment, comparable with that of Freud, than a number of illuminating conceptions about the ways in which an environmental situation can give rise to a devastating confusion. For instance, Bateson is responsible for the well-known 'double-bind' theory, which describes the effect on the child when parents communicate with him by means of simultaneous and incompatible verbal and non-verbal messages : for example, a mother may say, 'I love you darling', but the child knows by the turn of her mouth or the edge in her voice that she is possessed by an emotion which is very different from love.

The confusion theory has received its clearest and most forceful expression in a book by two British authors, Laing and Esterson, mentioned earlier.[6] These writers maintain that – at least in the case of families producing schizophrenic children – the parents invalidate the child's understanding of himself for the benefit of their own needs; there is a conflict between parents and child in which the former, in order to preserve their own (distorted) viewpoint, prevent the child from having access to the truth of his own perceptions. For instance, parents who despise each other may pretend to the child that their relationship is really one of the utmost trust and admiration. If the child were to notice and comment upon the fact that his father never took anything that his mother said seriously, the father might, in order to preserve the myth of harmony, deny the valid observations of the child, thereby undermining the latter's belief in his own understanding of the situation.

The devastating result of parental assumptions about their children is nicely depicted in Pinter's play, *A Night Out*, which describes the relationship between a widowed mother, Mrs Stokes, and her adult son, Albert. Mrs Stokes is intensely possessive and Albert is rather a mother's boy. He is meek enough until, halfway through the play, one of his mother's diatribes is more than he can endure :

MRS STOKES : . . . Yes. I don't say anything, do I? I keep quiet about what you expect me to manage on. I never grumble. I keep a lovely home, I bet there's none of the boys in your firm fed better than you are. I'm not asking for gratitude. But one thing hurts me, Albert, and I'll tell you what it is. Not for years, not for years, have you come up to me and said,

Mum, I love you, like you did when you were a little boy.
You've never said it without me having to ask you. Not since
before your father died. And he was a good man. He had
high hopes, he had, of you. I don't know what you do with
all your money. But don't forget what it cost us to rear you,
my boy, I've never told you about the sacrifices we made, you
wouldn't care, anyway. Telling me lies about going to the
firm's party. They've got a bit of respect at that firm, that's
why we sent you there, to start off your career, they wouldn't
let you carry on like that at one of their functions. Mr King
would have his eyes on you. I don't know where you've been.
Well, if you don't want to lead a clean life it's your lookout,
if you want to go mucking about with all sorts of bits of girls,
if you're content to leave your mother sitting here till mid-
night . . . the least you can do is sit down and eat the dinner
I cooked for you, specially for you, it's shepherd's pie.

Albert, after making a threatening gesture, leaves, and,
during the evening, meets a girl to whom he is crushingly
assertive in a manner which has been impossible for him in
his relationship with his mother. The play ends with a short
scene in which Albert returns home from his night out. He is
sitting in a chair, relaxed and triumphant.

Stretching his arms, he yawns luxuriously, scratches his head
with both hands and stares ruminatively at the ceiling, a smile
on his face. His mother's voice calls his name:
MOTHER (*from the stairs*) : Albert!
His body freezes. His gaze comes down. His legs slowly come
together. He looks in front of him.

During the harangue which follows, Albert remains slumped
in the chair and his mother's reproach turns to solicitude. She
strokes his hand :

We'll go away . . . together
Pause –
You're good, you're not bad, you're a good boy. . . .
I know you are . . . you are, aren't you?

With a fine accuracy of perception Pinter conveys the
bemused passivity of a son in the face of his possessive mother's

assumption that he is really the person she wants him to be. Albert, although he has at times been accused by his friends of being a mother's boy, has led an adjusted life, has surely never been to a psychiatrist. Now, in his momentary violent assertion or in his frozen apathetic state, he appears to be in the process of becoming a patient. Yet, paradoxically, we can see in this new, unfamiliar, and disturbing behaviour, an expression of health : perhaps for the first time in his life Albert is desperately seeking to express his real nature and true identity.

In *A Night Out*, we are drawn in sympathy towards the plight of the son. And so, in reading Laing and Esterson's book, or in being involved ourselves as psychotherapists[7] in such a family drama – we tend to side with the apparent 'patient' or 'victim'. What is happening to him – the complacent assumptions by the rest of the family that *his* viewpoint is wrong, the disintegration of his personality, the isolation in a mental hospital – outrages our sense of justice, leaves us with little capacity for a sympathetic understanding of the parents. Although this reaction is a natural – and even necessary – one, it can lead to a biased view of the ordinary confrontation between parent and child.

My own experience has left me in no doubt that certain families coerce their adolescent child into disbelieving his own perceptions, thoughts and feelings with such force that he becomes schizophrenic. To what degree such a child is predisposed to become schizophrenic is debatable. It seems likely that a family which has such a powerful capacity to undermine the adolescent has probably failed to provide the child, at an early age, with a strong sense of identity : in other words, the process is a cumulative one.

The mistake of Laing and – to a much greater degree – Cooper, is to use such tragic and horrifying cases as a basis for a theory of the family. Family life, however short of the sentimental ideal of the middle-class twentieth-century society, is not so deficient in meaning, truth and love as they paint it. Nor, I believe, are the confusions which lead to illness –

including schizophrenia – always the consequence of a ruthless (albeit unconscious), organized attempt to destroy the child's identity. It is often a more simple – more human – failure of understanding: an inability to confront the complexities and agonies of life. Let me give an example of what I mean.

Martin, a six-year-old boy, was referred to me at a Child Guidance Clinic as an emergency because, for the past ten days, he had been unable to separate from his mother, Mrs Jones. He had been with her every moment, day and night, even when she went to the toilet, and she was becoming exhausted and depressed. It was clear that they must be separated, and I arranged for Martin to be seen by a social worker while I talked to the mother. During his hour with the social worker, Martin was at first violent and self-destructive, to an alarming degree; then he stood in front of a mirror and screamed for a long time, shouting abuses at his mother. During the course of the session he said, 'I am my mother . . .', 'I am not my mother . . .', 'I am excited . . .', 'I don't eat anything . . .'. Gradually he calmed down, and later rejoined his mother and embraced her lovingly, saying 'I love you Mummy'; 'you don't leave people'. His mother's response to him seemed to me to lack directness – it had an element of the bedside manner about it.

The immediate cause of this crisis had been Mrs Jones's first consultation with a psychiatrist, in which it had been brought home to her that Martin was seriously disturbed and had the apparent mental age of a child of two or three years old. This was an unbearable shock to her (and – either through her anxiety about him or because of what he himself picked up from the psychiatric interview – to Martin).

The mother was a warm, intelligent person, who found it very difficult to trust others and who blew hot and cold in a way that I found confusing. She was, however, able, over the course of several months, to tell me a great deal about her own history and personal relationships.

Mrs Jones had herself always lacked a firm sense of her own value. Her own mother had only married her father because she had become pregnant, and had never really loved him. Thus she herself had been the object of her mother's affections and she was allotted the special task of making her mother happy – a commitment which still existed. By contrast her father was harsh to her, presumably jealous of her close tie to his wife, and undermined her confidence. Whereas her mother idealized her, believing there could be no limit to her attainments, her father took the ground from under her feet. As a result she found it extremely difficult to assess her own capabilities. This uncertainty was accentuated firstly because her mother believed in the supernatural powers of a 'guardian angel' who would shield the family from the hazards of the real world – a belief which she passed on to her daughter; secondly because there was fear of insanity in the family. Mrs Jones's grandfather died from cerebro-syphilis, and it was believed (by the Jones family) that this could be passed on, silently as it were, and emerge without warning in later generations. It was not surprising that she had always had a fear of insanity.

Before Martin was born Mrs Jones was tormented by fear that he would be abnormal. These apprehensions, stemming in part from her belief – medically unsupportable in this case – that he would be a victim of congenital syphilis, were magnified by the fact that her first son had been born dead. When Martin was born – a healthy baby – the hypochondriacal anxiety from which she had previously suffered on her own account dramatically disappeared, only to be replaced by anxiety over Martin. It was of crucial importance to her that he be a perfect baby, and she lived in constant fear that there might be something wrong with him. He was her first live male child and he was everything that she could have asked for. She could not believe her luck. Could such good fortune last? He was, in her husband's words to me, the apple of their eye. There was something so endearing about him that neither of the parents could bring themselves to be harsh with him.

This state of affairs continued until Martin was two years old, when external circumstances forced a period of excessive strain upon the family. At this time Mrs Jones was too harassed to give Martin the quality of attention which he had come to expect. He became a 'difficult' child, demanding and frightened. A couple of years later, it was clear to some people that he was not developing intellectually as he should, but his mother did not seem to notice this (and I believe that she had to deny it owing to her excessive anxiety about mental abnormalities of any kind).

The (tentative) diagnosis of mental subnormality made by the psychiatrist was the last straw. Denials were broken down and Mrs Jones's worst fears confirmed. This uncertainty about whether Martin was 'normal' or not was a constant pre-occupation; it 'nearly drove her crazy', dominated my discussions with her and was, I think, the reason for the bedside manner towards Martin that I had noticed in the first interview.

The preoccupation with mental illness was, however, no less noticeable in Martin than in his mother. He asked her time and time again, 'Is Martin all right, Mummy?' (he usually referred to himself in the third person), 'Is Martin ill?' 'Are you ill, Mummy?' 'Is Martin a nut-case, Mummy?', et cetera. Moreover, his behaviour also strongly suggested this preoccupation. He gave the impression much of the time that he was acting the part of a mad child. It is a difficult thing in practice – and perhaps in theory – to distinguish between the madness that is confusion and the adoption of a mad role, but it did seem that Martin was continually testing out his mother's response to apparently mad behaviour (wild laughing, pulling faces, falling about, shouting outrageous comments) particularly in the presence of others. He would slyly glance to see how his mother was taking it. He was worse if anyone watched him or talked about him in his presence, and this wild behaviour reached its height during and after the many psychiatric interviews he underwent (in which, presumably, he realized that the psychiatrist was trying to assess whether he was mentally ill or subnormal).

Time and time again in our discussions, Mrs Jones returned to the time of the family crisis, when Martin was two years old. It was at this point, she felt certain, that something went wrong : she lost contact with Martin. I believe her to be right. For reasons of discretion I cannot give an account of this crisis. It affected Mrs Jones in two ways : her attention was forced away from Martin, and her handling of Martin was criticized (unrealistically – that is, for neurotic reasons in others) in a way which undermined her confidence in her own way of relating to him. If she had been more secure she might have been able to withstand this attack on her judgement. The consequences of the loss of contact can be viewed in more than one way.

Firstly, Martin felt rejected and angry : the sudden loss of a close empathic relationship constituted a trauma. Whether this, in itself, was sufficient to cause illness in a child not unduly sensitive is doubtful.

Secondly, his mother, aware that something had failed between them, predisposed to anxiety and guilt over such a failure, over-compensated. In attempting to heal the wound she became preoccupied with Martin in an unhealthy way : she watched over him and worried about him too much. In Martin's words, years later : 'You flood me, Mummy.' Furthermore, her feelings of guilt and her sensitivity to his arrested emotional development inhibited her from disciplining him in a way that would have enabled him to perceive the natural limits of his aims. His internalization of her uncertainty about his capabilities showed itself in the way he sometimes talked to himself. One day I heard him having a conversation with himself in two quite different voices, one of which was unmistakably his mother's :

Mother (harshly emphatic) : 'Of *course* you can dress yourself, Martin. You know very well you can. You must dress yourself. You're a big boy now.'

Martin (in a small, uncertain voice) : 'Can he really dress himself ?'

Mother : 'You *can* go to school, Martin. You've got to behave like other children.'

Martin : 'Can he *really* go to school ?'

Different interpretations could be placed on this interchange. It might, for instance, be thought that the mother was – perhaps justifiably – being disciplinarian and that Martin was opposing her by assumed passivity. But the tones of voice suggested confusion and uncertainty: the mother overcompensating for her doubts and Martin genuinely bewildered. Because there was a confusion in his mother's mind over the question as to whether he was a separate person (she believed she had a mystical identification with him) and whether he was normal or abnormal, insane or a genius (for she attributed to him, perhaps with justification, an unusual perceptiveness) Martin could not establish a stable and realistic sense of his own identity. This made him ask such questions as: 'Is he Martin? Is he his mother? Will he grow up to be a lady?' and he had to adopt all manner of complicated manœuvres in order to find out what his mother *really* thought of him, why she thought it, and whether she was right; he needed to see beyond her words, to undermine her composed 'stereotyped' responses; to trick, shock or bully her into the truth at whatever risk to either of them.

The features which I have described derive from Martin's relationship with his mother – her doubts about him, her undue attentiveness, her inconsistent response to his aggression, et cetera – but I have largely omitted from this description the contemporary pressures on the mother (by family, neighbours and psychiatrists) which lessened her capacity to relate realistically to Martin, and to other influences, in home and school on Martin himself. In my description I have tried to identify three causal factors, amongst the many likely ones: firstly, an intense but fearful love for a child who seemed to promise everything, whose very preciousness aroused excessive anxiety in a mother who could not take her good fortune on trust; secondly, a traumatic event at two years of age; thirdly, a progressive loss of psychological contact between mother and child following the trauma. This progressive alienation had itself two components: the vicious circle of ever-widening discrepancy of response (for example, over-protection →

passivity → over-protection . . .) and the increasing extremities of perception (for example, is he mindless . . . is he a genius) which occurs when realistic judgement fails.

I have isolated these factors out of a situation which was enormously complex – more so than I have been able to describe and more so than I could ever know, and I have not discussed the possibility that unknown physiological factors may have contributed to the origin of Martin's problems. But even what little I did learn suggested to me that a theory which would attribute the illness either to the child's need to defend himself from reality or the parent's need to confuse him is an oversimplification.

To complete this discussion of the ways in which a child may be confused in assessing his potentialities I must now consider in more detail what happens when he is led to *over-estimate* the possibilities of experience.

How does this happen? The question is complicated by the psychoanalytic belief that even a healthy child in a good environment harbours undue and excessive expectations, is possessed by 'oral' wishes to 'devour' experience and to gain 'omnipotent' control of those around him. But there is no reason – except adult prejudice – to suppose that a child has such in-built greedy urges, that he consistently over-estimates what the world offers, that he does not accept natural limitations. Sleep is a natural limitation of wakefulness, yet he accepts this in the same way as he accepts the end of sleeping. Much of his behaviour which is often considered to be 'demanding' can be attributed to a search for reality. How else can a child test out the limits of possibility other than by pushing them until a sufficiently decisive resistance appears? Until the limit is reached, his expectations are *uncertain* rather than excessive, and when it is reached he is often surprisingly content to accept it, provided it has been reached in a meaningful way.

There is no doubt, however, that some children (and adults) may have outrageously greedy expectations of life. This is to be expected if a child has been unduly frustrated (aroused, only to be disappointed) and subsequently over-compensates,

E

like a hungry man after a famine. It will also occur if possibilities are presented to the child in an unrealistic way. There is a sense in which one cannot give too much to a child: a reasonable and appropriate response to him cannot be improved upon. But the child may be presented with an inappropriate and unbalanced environment which fosters the development of undue expectations in some ways, causing him to become addicted to certain stereotyped responses: for example, he may be kissed, fed or praised, and so on, to a degree that is ultimately unsatisfying, limiting and boring, but upon which he comes to depend as an expected right. This is the essence of spoiling: children treated in this way become convinced that they are specially privileged, and will strive with great ingenuity and persistence to persuade others of the validity of their requirements. If they can find a special and exalted place in society (for instance, leader, film star) they will not seem ill. Sometimes, they may seek in desperation, the ambiguous privileges of a sick role.[8,9]

Another hazard for the child who sees possibilities where they do not exist is the difficulty of making a selection. In ordinary circumstances a healthy person is not unduly taxed by the necessity of making choices. If, as with Martin, his environment contains too many uncertainties and ambiguities, or if, because of the way the concept of choice is presented to him, he comes to believe that there are more possibilities open to him than is really the case, he may become unable to deal with the sheer complexity of the problem; like an overworked computer he may break down by being fed with too many data. In a very interesting paper[10] McReynolds suggests that an excessive amount of perceptual data – a greater amount than can be assimilated – can be a cause of anxiety and contribute to schizophrenia. The reasons he puts forward for the difficulty of assimilating new information are that it comes in too fast or is too novel for the person to fit it in with what he already knows. In addition to these, I would suggest firstly an undue expectation as to what can be assimilated (failure to recognize one's limits), and secondly the need of some people to assimilate material into the 'false self system' (defensive organization) in addition to the healthy psyche.

McReynolds's approach is valuable in that it takes into consideration both the need to find meaning and the importance of mental energy, thereby attempting to relate the meaningful and mechanical elements in illness. He believes that the child needs to be in surroundings which are meaningful to him – which provide sufficient novelty and change to make life interesting. If, for some reason, the child's life fails to foster his wish to find meaning he will lack the stimulus to grow; if it forces him to attempt to make more sense out of it than is possible, he will disintegrate in the effort – unless, perhaps, he is able, through artistic creativity, to make sense of the excess material in a special area of his existence. (The situation is made more complicated – but not altered theoretically – by the fact that the child may later find the need to over-compensate; for instance, he may develop a false complexity to cover up a basic lack of meaning or an over-simplification to mask a subtle appreciation of life.)

The task of therapy is to show the person what he is, what he can become and what he can expect from others : to reveal both possibility and limitation. The theory upon which such therapy is based must not itself underestimate the person's capacity to search for and accept the truth about himself, and must be able to account for the failure of some people to find truth, without making the unwarranted assumption that their failure is due to inherited deficiency or innate tendency to evade truth.

At the same time, it must not give undue weight to the fact that some parents, in some ways, are not to be trusted. The parents' failure may have been crucial to the child and the latter's subsequent distrust of people may be natural and understandable. The therapist who comes to treat such a child (usually when he has become an adult) must be able to distinguish between the tragedy of this particular child's relationship with his parents and the kind of experience that is possible for more fortunate children. If the therapist takes up a too pessimistic view of human relationships – if he is influenced by a theory of family and society deduced from the worst elements of both – he may only confirm his patient's cynical belief that love does not exist. On specific occasions a therapist may have to take the side of the child against his parents, but a theory *based upon* such a stance will not be a true one.

8

The Practice of Psychotherapy

T'aint what you do, it's the way that
*   you do it;*
That's what gets results.
Pop Song

Let me first start with a declaration based on my experience as a psychotherapist.

People who come, of their own volition, to psychotherapy, do so for all sorts of conscious reasons: to rid themselves of pain, to understand themselves better, and so on. As the psycho-therapeutic situation develops, the crucial need of the patient is to be understood, valued, loved, respected by the therapist as an equal, fellow human being. This is irreducible, it is not simply transference. If the relationship goes well – if the two people grow to like, understand, respect each other – the patient will be helped. This fact subsumes anything else that can be said about psychotherapy. It is not something that I was led to expect by my training: rather it is a truth that has painfully been forced upon me by earlier failure.

What I am suggesting is not, of course, new. It has been said, in one way or another, explicitly or implicitly, by many psychotherapists before me[1,2]. Yet the message – even when pronounced by such influential workers as C. G. Jung, Sándor Ferenczi and Carl Rogers – has not been received. Today psychotherapy is considered a technique, a special process that can be taught; and the psychotherapist is expected to take up a detached attitude towards his patient.

Why should this be so? The main reason, I believe, is that the recognition of equality between therapist and patient is too threatening to the sense of identity of the former. Moreover, because Freud himself took up a detached position towards his patients (or at least, declared in his writings that he did so) the psychotherapist today who wholeheartedly holds the belief I am myself endorsing has to oppose himself on a radical issue against the greatest psychological genius of our time. It is a hard choice to make.

When Frau Anna O. – the celebrated patient – confronted Freud and Breuer with her powerful amorous needs, Breuer took fright, and left the patient – figuratively, if not literally – in the arms of Freud. Freud stayed with the patient and developed the technique of psychoanalysis. But is there a sense in which Freud took fright also? And is the technique of transference interpretation the manifestation of that fright? Freud, confronted by his patient's sexual desires, said, in effect, 'It is not me you desire; it is your father'; and thereby relieved himself from the anxiety which the situation – not surprisingly – aroused in him.

In his comprehensive study *The History of the Unconscious*, Ellenberger writes:

Certain features of psychoanalytic techniques can be understood in the context of what neuropathologists wrote at the end of the nineteenth century about the 'diabolical cleverness' of hysterics in deceiving the therapist and involving him in their games. It is as if each rule of Freudian technique was devised to defeat the cunning of these patients. The specific setting (the psychoanalyst's seeing without being seen) deprives the patient of an audience and of the satisfaction of watching the therapist's reactions.

The basic rule, together with the analyst's neutral attitude, prevents the patient from distorting words of the analyst, and places the latter in the position of a sensible parent who ignores the silly utterances of a little child. The rule that all appointments must be paid for, whether kept or not, and in advance, prevents the patient from punishing the therapist by absenteeism and non-payment. The analysis of transference as it occurs defeats the hysteric's concealed but always present aim: the seduction of the therapist.[3]

The fears of too deep an emotional involvement with, of exploitation, manipulation and seduction by, the patient which afflicted Breuer and Freud are still in evidence today. It has seemed to me, from my experience of psychotherapeutic training groups, that the kind of mistake which a practitioner most guards against, and about which he feels most shame, is to allow himself to be emotionally exploited. This is part of the ethos of our society: it is more shameful to confess that one has been taken for a ride than to admit undue scepticism.

Closely related to this is the fear of being 'unscientific'. In order to be heard, in order to feel justified in his beliefs, Freud had to place them in a theoretical framework as near to that of contemporary physical science as he could manage and to describe what he did as though it were an unemotional, technical procedure. And, today, psychotherapists are still under this pressure to conform.

A rather different reason for the psychotherapist's reluctance to describe his work in ordinary human terms is a kind of shyness. If I believe that the patient is helped by my own creatively human qualities – by my warmth, integrity, courage, strength, sensitivity, realism, honesty, et cetera – then it may appear rather immodest to say so. The implication is that I am better than other men. The Christians got out of this dilemma by saying: 'Not I, but my Father in Heaven . . . I am just a poor and worthless medium used by the Holy Spirit.'

The psychotherapist avoids it by saying: 'Not I, but the Technique'. Furthermore, an honest and complete description of what actually occurs in the consulting-room might well be embarrassing. To take a simple example. If a patient asks the therapist whether he is faithful to his wife and the therapist gives him an honest answer, it could be disconcerting to several people if the conversation was published. In reporting sessions psychotherapists often disguise the identity of their patients by changing factual details in a way which preserves the essential meaning of what took place. But I can hardly conceal my own identity and pretend it was really another therapist who was doing this work. One is up against the kind of problems which make true autobiographies so difficult to write. And the matter does not end there. Even when I am prepared to reveal all that went on I might still require the genius of a Tolstoy if I am to do justice in print to the subtlety of the encounter. A tape-recorder is no answer to these problems for it cannot catch my thoughts – and I shall, in any case, unconsciously select for the benefit of the machine. I am not saying that the task is impossible and should not be under-taken, but that the difficulties of true presentation are greater than is commonly supposed and account, to some extent, for the stereotype of case-history to be found in psychiatric and psychotherapeutic books and journals. Moreover, the less the therapeutic encounter is structured by technical procedures, the more testing is the task of reporting it with truth and accuracy.

If, as I am suggesting, it is the human qualities rather than technical know-how which are the effective agents in psycho-therapy, one is faced with an awkward question : why should these qualities of the therapist be more effective in helping the patient than those of his friends and relations? While noting, in parenthesis, that relatives and friends can indeed play a major part in healing and that psychotherapists are by no means always successful in their efforts to heal, I would sug-gest the following two reasons :

Firstly, the therapist is placed in a position calculated to evoke the best in him. A need for help has been identified. (Clinical situations in which no such need is apparent carry a less hopeful prognosis.) In a potentially fruitful therapeutic situation the patient has asked for help and the therapist is not encumbered by involvement in a confusion or power-struggle of long standing. He accepts psychological illness as an ordinary fact of life and in doing this he often supplies an environment which has been denied to the sick person. He is not dismayed or guilty or affronted or ashamed if his patient is ill – as a close relative may be. He is given, again in potentially fruitful encounters, the time and the freedom from extraneous interruptions and demands to devote himself to the patient and his problems. His circumstances are markedly different from, say, that of a mother whose baby needs her attention when another child has just cut his finger, the telephone is ringing and she is behind with the rent. I suggest that the so-called objectivity, detachment and non-involvement of the psychoanalyst is no more than his capacity to *focus* on the patient.

Secondly, the therapist is experienced in treating sick people. He has learned something of the way in which human anguish manifests itself and the sort of response that is needed to help. He is accustomed to looking for the truth that is concealed. But his experience, his aims, and his methods are not essentially different from those of the majority of mankind in ordinary situations in which people engage one another. He is more practised in his particular field of interest than most, but his skills are not necessarily esoteric. Nor is there any guarantee that even after years of work he is more gifted in the interpretation of minimal signs than many a person who does not even know what the word psychotherapist means. In so far as the psychotherapist is helped by his training this is primarily (as I suggested in Chapter I) because it reveals to him – or should do – some of the ways in which he characteristically fails to be truly and ordinarily himself when confronted by someone who is in distress.

We are now faced with a rather arduous problem. The richest source of our knowledge of mental illness has been Freud's technique of psychoanalysis – a method which sets the therapist apart from his patient in an attitude of scientific detachment. How can one account for this fact without abandoning belief in a humanistic approach to psychotherapy (if that is the right word for it)?

Much of Freud's achievement lay in his discovery of the degree to which childhood experience continues to live on in the adult and affect his attitude to others. In particular Freud noted and spelled out the ways in which a patient transfers early assumptions about people on to the therapist. Transference is the corner-stone of contemporary psychotherapeutic method. It is the means by which the therapist learns things about the patient which the latter cannot tell him in words.

In order to understand what is being transferred on to him, the therapist must avoid a blind unreflective response to his patient; he needs to observe these inappropriate assumptions about himself, and relay them back to the patient. Freud regarded this undertaking as a technique: partly, I imagine, because it seemed to him – and still more to those around him – an extraordinary business, remote from the usual means people devise for understanding one another, and partly because, as a scientist, he inevitably thought of his work as a technical procedure. Moreover, in order to use and explore his new discovery – the emergence of past patterns in present relationships – he had to focus his attention on this phenomenon to a degree which required him to adopt a detached attitude to his patients: to make a technical rather than an ordinary approach to them.

But do we still need to think of transference interpretation as an extraordinary procedure requiring a detached attitude to the other? Once a new insight has been made it gradually becomes assimilated into our ordinary appreciation of life. The originator in art and science changes our vision. What once required a special effort of understanding, and could not be reached by many, is now taken for granted. As Neville Cardus tells me in this morning's paper, Schoenberg's piano concerto will one day seem rather similar to Grieg's. Freud showed us the way, but it is a path on which now many unthinkingly follow, noting the ways in which we unknowingly betray our hidden feelings and transfer our childhood conflicts on to each other. Not that we were entirely in ignorance before. It must be a long time ago that a woman first said to a man: 'You treat me as if I were your mother'; but she would now be more likely to spell it out in detail.

But even if this argument is accepted may it not still be necessary for the therapist, if he is to permit the emergence of, and utilize, the transference, to adopt an attitude of scientific detachment, as psychoanalytic theory maintains? I suggest that the answer to this is 'No'.

At first sight it would appear reasonable to suppose – on an analogy with the cinema – that the nearer the therapist approaches the identity of a blank screen, the more easily he will evoke the projection on to himself of undistorted images by the patient. But in personal relationships a 'blank screen' response carries with it a negative emotional charge which must of necessity affect the attitude of the patient. An apparent *lack* of emotional response by a therapist is more likely to evoke a standard set of reactions in most patients: hurt, anger, withdrawal, confusion, idealization and envy of a being who seems to be so free of the emotional disturbances which afflict him and the people he knows in his ordinary life. Such reactions are artifacts caused by the therapeutic setting, rather than pure manifestations of childhood experience.

When the 'blank screen' of the therapist is depicted in this way it may be thought that I am drawing a caricature: presenting the picture of a certain kind of therapist, who, by reason of his own obsessionality, or because he has taken Freud's admonitions too literally, has turned himself into an inhuman computer. But I do not mean to limit myself to such cases, for I believe that the whole climate of opinion that has grown from Freud tends to inhibit emotional reciprocity in the warmest of therapists, so that it is only with the greatest of reluctance, if at all, that he can allow himself to reveal the feelings which the patient arouses in him.

This brings to mind a comment made to me by a patient recently. We were discussing her obsessional tendency to compartmentalize her experiences, and, in particular, how she maintained very strictly the professional doctor–patient relationship with me. She is herself the wife of a psychoanalyst and she went on to say: 'I don't see how we can be the same sort of people, as friends are. I have heard my husband on the telephone with patients. He has a special voice for them : he holds back. I can tell immediately whether he is talking to a patient or a friend.'

Transference manifestations occur – as is well-known – in ordinary living and are not inhibited by spontaneous emotional responses in others: we all repeat, in a stereotyped manner, certain patterns from our past. These patterns will not be observed unless the people concerned are alerted to the possibility of their existence, but being alerted does not mean they have to suppress their emotional responses. Contrary to the classical view, it would seem that an ordinary natural attitude to the patient provides a setting in which inappropriate responses, caused by childhood traumas, are more easily detectable. For example, unhappy childhood experiences tend to leave a person with negative beliefs about himself (although, of course, over-compensation may develop). It will be easier for him to reveal these painful feelings if he is able to perceive, believe and accept the real, positive, reactions of the therapist. (I am assuming that the therapist's overall feeling towards the patient is more likely to be positive than negative.)

One of the ways in which the contemporary psychotherapist adopts an attitude of detachment is his excessive tendency to *interpret* the patients' behaviour; for instance : 'You seem to be thinking of me as though I were an over-protective mother.' This method of calling attention to the phenomenon is not necessarily the most appropriate or useful. The therapist's response as a person may well carry more conviction : a spontaneous emotional reaction – 'Look, it's your *own* bloody life isn't it? You'll be expecting me to change your nappies next!' – may help to avoid the defensive tendency to regard the psychotherapeutic procedure as a kind of intellectual game (if we assume, of course, that the emotional reaction of the therapist is genuine and not a technical contrivance).* Excessive

---

* I refer here only to the manifestation of *appropriate* anger. It would be as irrelevant or harmful to castigate a truly regressed patient for not going out to work as to shout at a three-year-old child for being unable to write a letter.

preoccupation with verbal interpretation has led to neglect of other factors in the relationship which may be helpful.

There is another point. In believing that his capacity to help lies in his knowledge of a technique, the therapist places the patient in a passive position and minimizes the contribution which the latter makes to the endeavour. In particular, he is likely to work on the assumption that, because of his technical mastery, his own views of the interaction are right, the patient's wrong. This accounts for the very great emphasis placed on the patient's 'resistance' to interpretations. The concept of 'resistance' is based on the belief that the psychoanalyst's interpretations are correct and that if the patient is unwilling to accept them it is because they are painful to him; in other words, the determining factor in the state of resistance is avoidance of truth on the part of the patient.

It seems likely, however – and this thought follows from the line of argument pursued throughout this book – that the patient is concerned with pursuing truth at least as much as with avoiding it. He needs, therefore, to try to establish whether the therapist is himself in possession of truth and in so doing he may need to question the therapist with a degree of vigour that the latter may interpret as resistance unless he understands the encounter as one between equals who are searching for truth. Even when the patient's challenge to the therapist's viewpoint is unreasonable this may originate less in an avoidance of pain than in a compulsive doubt of any interpretation owing to confusion in his early life.

The crucial factor in the therapist's behaviour will in that case be the creation of an atmosphere of mutual trust, respect and flexibility in which the patient can feel safe to explore the truth. In such an atmosphere both participants can learn and dogmatic mistakes will be minimized: where the therapist may differ from his patient is in his belief that such an atmosphere is possible and helpful.

The assumption that psychotherapy is a technique, that the patient is a passive object in a process, known to the therapist, which takes place in a predictable way over a period of time is often made by patients and can be used defensively to maintain the neurosis. The following is an example.

Mr G., an intelligent man of forty-five, had a successful career, but having been helped a great deal by his father in the early stages, he never felt the success was his own, and lacked a sure sense of active identity. He was convinced that I had, in my mind, a detailed map of the course of his therapy to which he must conform. Naturally, I had, so he thought, to keep an emotional distance from him in order that I could keep my plan firmly in mind and observe how well or badly he was adapting to it. He accepted this régime gladly : it was inevitable and not at all distasteful to him.

However, one day he told me he had just been to a lecture by a man who fitted everything intellectually in its place precisely but was so involved in doing this that he failed to contact the audience. This led him to remember how his father knew the exact place of everything in the house, so that if he, Mr G., took a book out of a book-case, his father would immediately know what had been taken and would question him about it. He remembered the pain and anger aroused by such a close, controlling observation and was then able to recognize his (previously unconscious) dissatisfaction with the passive acceptance of my know-how, an acceptance which he had assumed was required of him.

A patient's hopeful expectations of help from the therapist enable him to make what is sometimes referred to as a 'working alliance'; he is able to make the attempt to change in the context of his hopes and the therapist's hopes for him. In certain cases, and perhaps to some extent in all cases, this trust in the therapist leads to the situation – to which I have referred in earlier chapters – known as 'holding' the patient : a milieu and medium is provided in which he can give up his pretences of functioning adequately and can explore, imagine and develop rather in the way in which a baby can grow in the presence of a mother who supports but does not unduly impinge.

The value of the concept of holding lies not only in the

recognition that some patients at some times need a protective care which will allow them to be and grow, but also in the observation, which Winnicott makes, that in such circumstances the analyst must act spontaneously. He thus advocates a departure, not only from a particular technique, but from anything that could be *called* a technique. This refers to certain moments in a developing relationship of trust in which the desperate need of the patient to break through a barrier can only be met if the therapist himself feels a corresponding emotional response and acts upon it. Such moments are, I think, very difficult to set down in words, for the essence of the experience lies in the closeness of feeling between the two people rather than in anything they may say or do. And it will be quite different in nearly all respects when two other people are concerned. But, in the hope that I shall not lose all in the telling, I shall give an example of what I mean.

Joyce was a young woman in her twenties. During the sessions with me she experienced herself and the world as almost totally disintegrated. Her perception of herself, myself and the consulting-room was not stable. She lay on the couch throughout each session, in abject terror, trembling all over. Nothing felt real. The ceiling seemed to be falling down upon her, she seemed to be falling and she lived in a kind of nightmare in which her existence was, at every moment and in every way, threatened.

I interpreted to her what this seemed to mean : in particular, that she was experiencing or re-experiencing a very primitive infantile insecurity. I also reassured her, saying that I myself did not live in this nightmare and that I would not abandon her to it.

At the end of each session – with one exception when she fell to the floor – she managed to integrate herself sufficiently well to 'survive' until the next session. But, in spite of this and the basic optimism I felt about her, I found her therapy a strain and a worry.

One day she seemed physically even more agitated than usual and was holding her arms out above her.

I said, 'You are wanting to hold on to somebody?'

'Yes.'

'Do you want to hold on to me?'

'Yes, I do.'

I went over to her and she clutched hold of my arms with urgent and desperate intensity. After a while she quietened a little. 'That's the nicest thing anyone has ever done to me,' she said. She continued to hold on to me throughout the session and again the next session. At one point she noticed that I was feeling uneasy. I agreed, and tried to tell her why, apologizing for my inhibitions, but not feeling satisfied with this explanation. Shortly after this she withdrew her hand, without apparent anger and said, 'It doesn't feel right now.' This breach between us was intolerable to me at that moment and I took back her hand, saying, 'Is it all right if *I* do this?' She answered, 'Yes; people need to touch each other.' There was something in the way she expressed, simply and directly, this obvious truth, that released me from my inhibition. I felt enriched by what she said and no longer ill at ease.

Afterwards I was able to formulate to myself more exactly the unease I had felt. It derived from the question: 'What am I doing holding her hand? Am I a therapist applying a technique or am I just doing this?' What had started as a spontaneous response had become, for me, a considered procedure. It was not until she had assured me that it was perfectly natural that I was able to see this simple truth myself.

In the following session she said, somewhere near the beginning, 'I like your jumper.' My jumper was, in fact, rather similar to her own; both were past their prime, the sort of garment one knocks about the house in. I said, 'I think you like it because it makes you feel that I am just ordinary, that we are alike'; and she agreed. Soon afterwards, however, she said, 'But I don't feel close enough to you.' I did not think that she meant this in a physical sense, so I suggested that it was because she knew so little about me and my life. For the remainder of the session she asked me questions about myself which I answered as fully and truthfully as I could.

After the session she stood up and said, in the emphatic way she reserved to convey something important to me: 'Thank you *very* much for telling me about yourself.'

She started the next session by saying: 'I'm terribly afraid that you might look at me and say, "I don't know who you are. I've never seen you before." '

Myself: 'Did you feel we knew each other last time, when I talked about myself?'

Joyce: 'Yes, much more than usual.'

Myself: 'Shall we go on with that?'

Joyce: 'Yes, I'd like to.'

Throughout this session, I again talked about myself and this time I quite lost myself in the telling of it, revealing some of my deepest anxieties. I felt none of my earlier uneasiness with her. I find it difficult to formulate what was happening between us in terms of a psychotherapeutic procedure. What was striking, however, was that Joyce was calm and contained in contrast to her usual state of agitated disintegration and was able to ask me questions and respond to me in a very natural and easy way. That, to some extent at least, I was revealing my frailty and my similarity to her did not appear to disturb her nor reduce her confidence in my ability to help. And in the following session she was able to reveal her despair more coherently than ever before.

What gave Joyce comfort was, I think, not only that I 'held' her in a way that made her feel safe but that I did so in a way that made her feel that we were essentially similar beings.

The kind of interchanges I have described were often repeated and we had to understand which inhibitions were inherently mine, and which occurred because she was unconsciously manoeuvring me to repeat her mother's failures of handling when she was a baby – yet desperately needing me to avoid these failures. It was not, however, until circumstances outside the consulting-room forced me to 'hold' her in a different sense – to show that I was prepared to treat her in spite of strong opposition from others – that she really began to get better and to grow as an independent person. And even then our relationship continued essentially on the same lines. What made her feel safe and become more real was my spontaneous warmth. On the occasions when I held back – when a gesture or affectionate word failed to pass my censor – she became frightened and saw *me* as 'not real: just a collection of pieces stuck together'.

One day the session took place, as it sometimes did, outside. We sat on the lawn, talked of various things, then Joyce asked me – a recurrent question – 'Do you like me?' I said: 'Yes, of course.' We fell into silence. I began to be uneasy, had nothing to say, and felt an urge to put my arm round her and stroke her rather in the way that she was now stroking my dog, but I was too embarrassed to do this in full view of the neighbours. Suddenly she said: 'I'm frightened here! Can we go back inside?' I said 'Yes', put my arm round her, and we returned to the consulting-room where she cuddled up to me like a small child. 'I was so frightened,' she said. 'All the flowers were going into little pieces and nothing was real.' At the end of the session she turned to me and said: 'You've helped me today.'

What occurred between Joyce and me in this session was both spontaneous and shared; we were moved by it and felt close to each other. It was, I think, the only thing which could have happened of any real value at the time and it was only of value because there was nothing contrived about it.

I am not suggesting that touching the other person or revealing one's weaknesses to him are necessary or useful methods in psychotherapy: to do so would reduce spontaneous and emotional interchanges – of whatever kind – to mere technique. I would rather put it that natural responses, as occur in ordinary life, are sometimes of crucial importance to therapy and this is particularly the case when people reveal their true and vulnerable selves.

In so far as holding is a departure from technique, it is wrought out of the urgency and desperation of certain patients who, at certain times, cannot tolerate technique. But should it be left to desperation to provoke a human response? Does one need to be parched with thirst before drink is provided?

Winnicott tried very hard to present his findings in the accepted psychoanalytical tradition. This has perhaps helped towards a wide professional hearing, but it has been done at a cost. His most valuable work is seen as an extension of, or departure from, a psychoanalytic technique which remains, in most circumstances, the recommended approach. He even suggests that a psychoanalyst should not attempt such a departure until he has ten years experience of routine psychoanalytic practice behind him. I would put it another way: it takes ten years for most psychoanalysts to gain the confidence to depart from a technical approach which they never should have adopted in the first place.

What, then, is psychotherapy? What relationship does technique bear to the encounter between the two people concerned? Is it perhaps comparable to the significance of sexual technique in the experience of physical love? A diagram of coital positions may help performance, but it omits the true meaning of the relationship and, if invested with a mistaken meaning, will confuse and corrupt.

The practice of psychotherapy can be categorized in several different ways: as a science (the important factor is a technique which can be taught); as an art (technique, although it may be considered important, is secondary to creative inspiration); as a relationship (similar to that between parent and child, husband and wife, friend and friend: technique is of marginal importance). To my mind, while the second of these alternative formulations is more appropriate than the first, the third comes nearest to the truth. But one must consider, more closely, the nature of technique.

According to the *Oxford English Dictionary* a technique is:

a manner of artistic execution or performance in relation to formal or practical details (as distinct from general effect, expression, sentiment etc. . . .); mechanical skill in artistic work.

But of course, the word has been extended to areas of life beyond the realm of what is commonly understood as art. The chief significant characteristics of a technique are, I suggest, as follows:

Firstly, a technique is mechanical, in the sense meant in the definition given by the *Oxford English Dictionary* above: it stands in contrast to imagination.

Secondly, a technique is applicable to known, repeatable phenomena. It is inappropriate for use in human situations in which one is presented with that unique and unpredictable entity – a person.

Thirdly, a technique is resorted to as an inferior alternative when spontaneous behaviour is impossible. This may occur when a natural personal response is too disturbing to either person in a relationship, in which case a defensive manoeuvre takes place.

Fourthly, a technique cannot be taken for granted as part of the equipment of people which enables them to fulfil the ordinary undertakings of their lives (an ability which develops naturally unless inhibited), but must be learned from a specialist in a certain branch of knowledge.

Fifthly, there is, however, a special circumstance in which a way of relating to people may, with some justification, be referred to as a technique. This occurs when a natural form of experiencing life and relating to people has, for some reason, been forgotten by a culture. To take an example: if a society forgot that maternal love was a natural and inevitable part of human experience, mothers would have to be taught how to look after their babies and what they were taught might be called, by that society, a technique (perhaps our own society goes some way towards demonstrating this possibility). Such a technique would, of course, be no substitute for love; but, as an emergency measure, it would probably have some value.

How many of those procedures which have come to be thought of as techniques are really natural modes of relating which have atrophied on our society? The feature of contemporary psychotherapy which is the most striking and most at variance with ordinary personal behaviour is the interpretation of what Freud referred to as unconscious experience. To the extent that the recognition of this 'forgotten language' was the most significant feature of Freud's contribution, his work should be considered as a technique, in the sense of a method to rehabilitate a lost mode of experience. But if the approach to the patient, known as psychotherapy, to which Freud's work gave such enormous impetus, is viewed as merely an extension of this technique, the encounter becomes dehumanized and therefore crippled, for the degree to which one perceives a person as a person is likely to vary inversely with technical procedures used for handling him. Moreover – as I suggested earlier – when Freud's rediscovery finds its way into contemporary thought, the specialized methods of psychoanalysts designed to uncover its manifestations lose their particularity.

In sum, what I am trying to show is that psychotherapy is primarily an ordinary interpersonal activity, and the special technical procedures to which psychotherapists resort are, at best, of secondary importance, and, at worst, inhibiting factors. The belief that it is primarily a technique is, to a large extent, a defensive manoeuvre – one that is subsumed by the contemporary scientific approach to human behaviour – designed to avoid the pain, risk and uncertainty of emotional involvement. Many of the procedures which are characteristic of psychotherapy – understanding, interpreting, holding, and so on – may occur in ordinary life and would be taken for granted by a healthy society – one less schizoid–obsessional, more attuned to the recognition of human feelings, than our own. And even our society – so ready to apply the label 'technique' – could hardly consider those qualities such as warmth, honesty, integrity without which a therapeutic endeavour is still-born, to be anything other than part of the ordinary business of creative living.

In pursuing one line of thought there is always a danger of underestimating – or, at least, of conveying the impression that one underestimates – other areas in the field that are significant.

I have been concerned to argue the neglected case for ordinary human values in the care of mentally disturbed people, and it may seem to the reader that I have not given due attention to the importance of technical procedures: of the study and control of the physiology of the organism, of the statistical assessment of individual and social factors, and of the interpretation of unconscious phenomena according to well-established schemes of thought. If in this book I have given little space to these factors it is not because I think them unimportant, but because I believe that the contemporary notion of scientific truth provides them with an exaggerated and misleading influence. But my deepest misgiving lies elsewhere. It is the fear that I have conveyed that the spontaneous and open psychotherapeutic approach is easy, or painless, or that I am, as a practitioner who believes that love helps patients, more blessed than others with the capacity to give it (and by 'love' I do not mean a sentimental attitude from which all iron has been extracted): or that I believe the chances of a therapist's being able to maintain positive feelings in the face of *persistent* rejection by the patient to be good. To put the matter in the form of a rhetorical question: how realistic is it to expect a psychotherapist to become deeply involved with a large number of anguished fellow beings without putting himself under too great a strain? My own experience – and that of colleagues with whom I have discussed this painful question – leads me to think that most of us can only do a certain amount of such work without an impoverishment of our lives. All occupations have their hazards. However, it is as well to recognize the existence of the hazard, and the limitation which it imposes not only upon a particular practitioner, but on the degree to which psychotherapy as a form of treatment can be expected to reduce the sufferings of the human race. But one can hope that the psychotherapeutic approach will eventually lessen the numbers of those who need intensive care, and engender a climate of opinion in which such care is more easily shared than at present.

Notes

CHAPTER 2

1. Lomas, P., 'The Significance of Post-partum Breakdown', in *The Predicament of the Family*, edited by Lomas, The Hogarth Press (1967).
2. Lomas, P., 'Taboo and Illness', *British Journal of Medical Psychology* (1969), 12, 33.
3. Laing, R. D., *The Divided Self*, Tavistock Publications (1960); also Pelican Books (1965).
4. Szasz, T. S., *The Myth of Mental Illness*, Hoeber-Harper, New York (1961).

CHAPTER 3

1. Piaget, J., *The Mechanisms of Perception*, translated by G. N. Seagrim, Routledge & Kegan Paul (1969).
2. Weber, M., quoted in Freund, J. *The Sociology of Max Weber*, Allen Lane The Penguin Press (1968).
3. Mandelstam, N., *Hope Against Hope*, Collins, Sons & Co., (1968).
4. Roszak, T., *The Making of the Counter Culture*, Faber & Faber (1970).
5. Leary, T., *The Politics of Ecstasy*, Paladin (1969).
6. Sarbin, T. H., 'Theoretical Perspectives', in *Changing Perspectives in Mental Illness*, ed. Stanley C. Plog and Robert B. Edgerton, Holt, Rinehart & Winston (1969).
7. Lomas, P., 'Ritualistic Elements in the Management of Childbirth', *Brit. J. Med. Psychol.* (1967) 39, 207.

8. Lafitte, P., *The Person in Psychology*, Routledge & Kegan Paul (1957).
9. Chertok, L., *Motherhood and Personality*, Tavistock Publications (1969).
10. Merleau-Ponty, M., *Phenomenology of Perception*, Routledge & Kegan Paul (1962).
11. Langer, S., *Mind: An Essay in Human Feeling*, The John Hopkins Press, Baltimore, Maryland (1967).

CHAPTER 4

1. Schachtel, E., *Metamorphosis*, Basic Books, New York (1959).
2. Suttie, I. D., *The Origins of Love and Hate*, Peregrine Books (1960).
3. Abraham, K., *Selected Papers of Karl Abraham*, The Hogarth Press and the Institute of Psychoanalysis (1927).
4. Fairbairn, W. R. D., *Psychoanalytical Studies of the Personality*, Tavistock Publications (1952).
5. Bowlby, J., *Attachment and Loss: Volume I: Attachment*, The Hogarth Press and the Institute of Psychoanalysis (1969).
6. Winnicott, D. W., *The Maturational Processes and the Facilitating Environment*, The Hogarth Press and the Institute of Psychoanalysis (1965).

CHAPTER 5

1. Lomas, P., 'Psychoanalysis – Freudian or Existential', in *Psychoanalysis Observed*, ed. Charles Rycroft, Pelican Books (1968).
2. Cooper, D., *The Death of the Family*, Allen Lane The Penguin Press (1971).
3. Holbrook, D., *Human Hope and the Death Instinct*, Pergamon Press (1971).
4. May, R., *Psychology and the Human Dilemma*, Van Nostrand Reinhold Co., Princeton, New Jersey (1967).
5. Rogers, C., *Client-Centered Therapy*, Freeman & Co. (1952).
6. Rogers, C., *Encounter Groups*, Allen Lane The Penguin Press (1971).
7. Boss, M., *Psychoanalysis and Daseinsanalysis*, Basic Books, New York (1963).

CHAPTER 6

1. Winnicott, D. W., *Collected Papers*, Tavistock Publications (1958).
2. Balint, M., *Primary Love and Psychoanalytic Technique*, The Hogarth Press (1952).
3. Milner, M., *The Hands of the Living God*, The Hogarth Press and the Institute of Psychoanalysis (1969).
4. Rycroft, C., *Imagination and Reality*, Hogarth, London (1968).
5. Khan, M. M. R., 'Regression and Integration in the Analytic Setting', *International Journal of Psychoanalysis* (1960) 41, 130, etc.
6. Langer, S., *Philosophy in a New Key*, Harvard University Press, Cambridge, Massachusetts (1960).
7. Freud, A., *The Ego and the Mechanisms of Defence*, The Hogarth Press (1937).
8. Klein, M., 'Notes on Some Schizoid Mechanisms' (1946), in *Developments in Psychoanalysis*, ed. Joan Riviere, The Hogarth Press (1952).
9. Bion, W. R., 'Language and the Schizophrenic', in *New Directions in Psychoanalysis*, ed. Melanie Klein, Paula Heimann and R. E. Money-Kyrle, Tavistock Publications (1955).
10. Woodmansey, A. C., 'The Internalisation of External Conflict', *Int. J. Psycho-anal.* (1966) 47, 349.

CHAPTER 7

1. Festinger, L., *Theory of Cognitive Dissonance*, Row, Peterson, Evanston (1957).
2. Fairbairn, W. R. D., *Psychoanalytic Studies of the Personality*, Tavistock Publications (1952).
3. Lidz, T., *The Family and Human Adaptation*, The Hogarth Press and the Institute of Psychoanalysis (1964).
4. Bateson, G., Jackson, D. D., Haley, J. and Weakland, J., 'Towards a Theory of Schizophrenia', *Behavioural Science* (1956) I, 251.
5. Lynn, W., Ryckoff, Day, Hirsch, 'Pseudomutuality in the Families of Schizophrenics', *Psychiatry* (1958) 21205.

6. Laing, R. D. and Esterson, A., *Sanity, Madness and the Family: Volume I: Families of Schizophrenics*, Tavistock Publications (1964); also Pelican Books (1970).

7. Lomas, P., 'Family Role and Identity Formation' *Int. J. Psycho-anal.* (1961) 42, 371.

8. Main, T. F., 'The Ailment', *Brit. J. Med. Psychol.* (1957) 30, 129.

9. Lomas, P., 'Family Interaction and the Sick Role', in *The Role of Psychosomatic Disorder in Adult Life*, ed. Wisdom and Wolff, Pergamon Press (1965).

10. McReynolds, P., 'Anxiety and Assimilation of Percepts', in *Aetiology of Schizophrenia*, ed. Don Jackson, Basic Books, New York (1960).

CHAPTER 8

1. Halmos, P., *The Faith of the Counsellors*, Constable & Co. (1965).

2. Steinzor, B., *The Healing Partnership*, Secker & Warburg (1968).

3. Ellenberger, H. F., *The Discovery of the Unconscious*, Allen Lane The Penguin Press (1970).

Index